Yours for the Asking

Yours for the Asking

Asking

An Indispensable Guide to Fundraising and Management

Reynold Levy

WILEY

John Wiley & Sons. Inc.

Published by John Wiley & Sons, Inc., Hoboken, New Jersey.

Published simultaneously in Canada.

For general information on our other products and services, or technical support, please contact our Customer Care Department within the United States at 800-762-2974, outside the United States at 317-572-3993 or fax 317-572-4002.

Wiley also publishes its books in a variety of electronic formats. Some content that appears in print may not be available in electronic books.

For more information about Wiley products, visit our Web site at http://*www.wiley.com*.

Library of Congress Cataloging-in-Publication Data:

Levy, Reynold.
    Yours for the asking: an indispensable guide to fundraising and management / Reynold Levy.
        p. cm.
    Includes bibliographical references and index.
    ISBN: 978-0-470-24342-8 (cloth)
    1. Fund raising. I. Title.
    HG177.L47 2008
    658.15'224—dc22

                                                                                    2008025017

For my wife, Elizabeth,
our children, Justin and Emily,
and my sister, Joyce:
You have given me all that an author
could possibly need—without my even asking.

CONTENTS

ALSO BY REYNOLD LEVY

N *earing the Crossroads: Contending Approaches to American Foreign Policy*

G *ive and Take: A Candid Account of Corporate Philanthropy*

ACKNOWLEDGMENTS

Writing a book while working full time at a demanding post is a challenge. It offers a sense of immediacy and engagement to the reader as the subject is very current and preoccupies the author in his "day job." It allows one to draw on real-life examples, to court controversy when necessary, and to compel reflection on professional practice.

Of course, writing this way also has its costs. Facing an unremitting deadline. Losing sleep. Forgoing vacations. Running the risk of not tempering the "here and now" enough with the "then and there."

I write this book out of a conviction that too few chief executives offer their views and perspectives when in office and, for that matter, after they leave. One reason to do it now is the reality that the failure to act in the present may, in fact, doom a project entirely. The unwritten manuscript is the bane of the curious professional and the avid student.

To my knowledge, no chief executive of any major nonprofit has written about fundraising and its influence—on the institution, on the donor, and on the professional and volunteer solicitor. This gap in the literature is significant given the fact that some $300 billion is now raised annually in America and for virtually any CEO an ability and willingness to raise funds has become a central requirement of his or her professional life.

What's more, I truly agree with Mahatma Gandhi that "the difference between what we do and what we are capable of doing would suffice to solve most of the world's problems." If the veritable army of this country's fundraisers performed their work more professionally, creatively, insistently, and resourcefully and if tens of thousands more volunteers were recruited to the task, the incremental funds raised could vastly strengthen our nation's problem-solving capabilities.

Cures for disease would be found more rapidly. The nation's educational performance at the primary and secondary school level would be improved more quickly. Utterly unnecessary deaths in our nation's hospitals from medical error would decline more swiftly. The doors to our colleges and universities would swing open wider to the working class and to the children of first-generation Americans.

The contribution of this nation's Third Sector to meeting such twenty-first-century challenges is constrained by a lack of resources. Acquiring them with a greater sense of urgency, of competency, and of creativity is a critical task. It can be accomplished, but only if the chief executive becomes personally engaged and catalyzes volunteers and professional staff with vision and by example.

My confidence about our collective ability to improve performance is rooted in respect for the qualities and accomplishments of today's leaders. They work hard and achieve much. But they can work smarter and accomplish much more. They number in the tens of thousands. Their ranks can grow exponentially. Those served by our nation's Third Sector deserve the very best we can be. "The fierce urgency of now" that drove Martin Luther King, Jr. is no small part of my inspiration.

To put pen to paper, motivation isn't enough. One needs supporters and friends.

No one has encouraged me to write more than Nessa Rapoport, a friend since my days at the 92nd Street Y, some 30 years ago, and herself an accomplished author of both fiction and nonfiction. Her gentle prodding serves as a kind of superego. When Nessa calls, she usually asks two questions: "What's on your mind?" and "Reynold, that sounds really important, have you written it down?" *Yours for the Asking* is one answer to both questions.

Nessa, thank you. Thank you very much.

Gratitude needs also to be expressed to my volunteer colleagues who have served as role models or worked at my side to strengthen, principally, the International Rescue Committee and Lincoln Center. The chairs of each, John Whitehead and Frank Bennack, and before him Beverly Sills and Bruce Crawford, respectively, from whom I've learned much, as you will discover. David Rubenstein, the founder of the Carlyle Group and chairman of Lincoln Center's Capital Campaign Steering Committee and its most active members, Katherine Farley, Peter Malkin, Rita Hauser, Blair Effron, Renee Belfer, Roy Furman, Barbara Block, Richard DeScherer, Joel Ehrenkranz, Tom Renyi, and Steve Ross, among them.

They and their colleagues follow in a tradition of the extraordinary leadership of the chairs of Lincoln Center with whom I was privileged to work—Martin E. Segal, Bruce Crawford, Beverley Sills and Frank Bennack. Their distinguished service and that of Nat Leventhal, the president of Lincoln Center for some seventeen years, set a high standard for what it means to govern and manage a major public trust like Lincoln Center.

More generally, I'd also like to acknowledge the unselfish acts of dozens of relatively new trustees at both the IRC and Lincoln Center. I participated in recruiting a cadre of gifted civic leaders, many in their 30s, 40s, or early 50s. They choose to spend more time in the boardroom than in the country club or on the golf course, and they offer ample treasure to the institutions and causes they help govern.

At both institutions this fresh class of trustees supplemented the energy, determination, and generosity of veterans. They will also supply the next generation of board leadership, assuring much-needed continuity.

I shall refrain from naming names. All are on the public record. Some have become good and cherished friends. One and all, they have my admiration and respect. It remains a privilege to work at their sides and call them partners in a common cause.

Among the many professions that have benefited enormously from the entry of women into the workplace over recent decades is fundraising. I've been blessed by many development directors and fundraising staff with whom to work. Three stand out. Rebecca Rosow at the 92nd Street Y. Janet Harris at the IRC. And Tamar Podell at Lincoln Center. Each brought distinctive strengths to their outstanding work. Each recruited and motivated gifted colleagues and determined volunteers. All were fun to be around and to learn from. I feel fortunate to have worked with them.

It is not only the author who "sacrifices" to write a book while shouldering other responsibilities. Two of my associates at Lincoln Center sacrificed spare time and serenity as well.

Tom Dunn, my principal assistant, raised his professional game and took on assignments that would have cost me precious hours or shielded me from the nice but unnecessary phone calls, meetings, and the like. He preserved a modicum of space for me to write and a semblance of sanity in my professional life. He knows how much I value him and our association.

Kristy Geslain typed every word of this manuscript with patience, attention to detail, and grace under pressure for which I am extremely grateful. Her high standards are matched by an even temperament, a rare combination.

Julie Woolard assisted Kristy with humor and energy.

A very good friend, Ed Bligh, read a late draft of the book cover to cover. He caught many mistakes and infelicities. *Yours for the Asking* is the beneficiary of his keen eye and editorial pen. I'm glad I summoned the courage to ask for his help.

I'm also grateful to friends and colleagues who read a version of the manuscript and offered helpful commentary: Alan Batkin, Tom Brokaw, Indra Nooyi, Tamar Podell, Lesley Friedman Rosenthal, David Rubenstein, Dan Rubin, Betsy Vorce, and John Whitehead.

One reader deserves a special acknowledgment. Bart Friedman, a senior partner of the firm Cahill, Gordon & Reindel, is my best friend. He brought to *Yours for the Asking* an appreciation for this precious Third Sector of ours and fervent desire to see it flourish. He's given me unstinting support in every important endeavor I have undertaken. I am blessed to have met him as a child and to have stayed in close touch ever since.

Of course, the team from John Wiley & Sons, headed by Susan McDermott, could not have been easier to work with or more encouraging. She and her colleagues are supportive resources any author would be privileged to have in their corner.

I'm also extremely pleased to record my thanks to those who helped create a fund for this book's dissemination. To John Ruskay and the Federation of Jewish Philanthropies, to Lance Lindblom and the Nathan Cummings Foundation, and to John Whitehead I offer a spirited expression of thanks.

My wife, Elizabeth, encouraged me to record my experience so that others might benefit. She is an extraordinary partner who shares my conviction about the importance of nonprofit institutions in America. She has spent much of her own professional life contributing to their vibrancy. This book is the beneficiary of her career, of her own careful review of the manuscript and of our life together.

I count myself a lucky guy.

Reynold Levy
June 2008

ABOUT THE AUTHOR

Reynold Levy is the president of Lincoln Center for the Performing Arts, the largest and most consequential institution of its kind anywhere in the world.

In earlier professional incarnations, Dr. Levy served as the president and chief executive officer of the International Rescue Committee (1997–2002), the senior officer of AT&T in charge of government relations (1994–1996), president of the AT&T Foundation (1984–1996), executive director of the 92nd Street Y (1977–1984), and staff director of the Task Force on the New York City Fiscal Crisis (1975–1977).

A graduate of Hobart College, Dr. Levy holds a law degree from Columbia University and a PhD in government and foreign affairs from the University of Virginia. Dr. Levy is currently a member of the Board of Overseers of the International Rescue Committee, a trustee and chairman of the Executive Committee of the Peterson Institute for International Economics, a member of the Council on Foreign Relations, and a board member of Third Way.

He has written extensively and spoken widely about philanthropy, the performing arts, humanitarian causes and issues, and the leadership and management of nonprofit institutions. Dr. Levy has been a senior lecturer at The Harvard Business School. He has also taught law, political science, and nonprofit administration at Columbia and New York universities and at the City University of New York.

Dr. Levy is the author of *Give and Take: A Candid Account of Corporate Philanthropy* (1999, Harvard Business School Press) and *Nearing the Crossroads: Contending Approaches to American Foreign Policy* (1975, Free Press of Macmillan). His speeches and essays have found their way into over a dozen books and anthologies and into leading newspapers. He frequently appears on radio and television.

Dr. Levy is married to Elizabeth A. Cooke. They have two children, Justin and Emily. All reside in New York City.

INTRODUCTION

Almost every American does it.

In 2007, the population of the United States gave $306 billion to charity. That sum represents 2.3 percent of the average American's disposable income. Two-thirds of all households contributed funds to nonprofit institutions. For each of the last five years, Americans donated more to their favorite organizations and causes than they saved for themselves. And of that total, corporations gave $15.7 billion, or about 1 percent of their pretax income.[1]

Giving is not a spontaneous act. People, corporations, and foundations donate funds largely because they are asked to do so.

It is a puzzle that while giving funds to nonprofit institutions is hardly unusual, the act of asking seems so universally disliked, misunderstood, and disdained. It is even more perplexing to discover that there is no must-read, must-own guide to raising funds, given the hundreds of thousands of Americans who struggle to solicit donations every day.

Yours for the Asking has been written for anyone who wishes to overcome the fear or simply the hesitation of asking friends and strangers for money. It is designed for those who wish to improve the effectiveness of their fundraising. It is motivated by the conviction that more charitable funds are available by orders of magnitude to prevent and cure disease, eliminate poverty, expand education, and relieve the misery of the bottom billion human beings who find themselves seemingly fated to occupy the lowest rung of the economic ladder.

The capacity and willingness of Americans to support nonprofit institutions has withstood the test of time.

Of course, when employment, gross domestic product, corporate earnings, and the stock market are rising at a vigorous pace, so, too, do the prospects for robust giving. But even when the U.S. economy falters, donations to charitable causes can remain vibrant.

After all, the case for many nonprofits strengthens as the economy weakens and as all levels of government experience expense budget cutbacks. For the poor among us, for the victims of recession, the Salvation Army, Catholic Charities, the Federation of Jewish Philanthropies, and Protestant Welfare Agencies and the local church and synagogue are an indispensable safety net. In rough economic patches, more Americans turn urgently for help to the vital services they provide. When jobs are cut, homes are foreclosed, and government assistance decreases, the need for compensatory charitable support is clear, present, and compelling.

For many Americans, the charitable act is habitual. It is performed through thick and thin. Built into our values, giving to organizations and causes we care about becomes an integral part of our lives. Central to our identity, philanthropy comes naturally.

For the affluent, paying for charitable gifts tends to emanate from accumulated assets, not annual income. The rich don't donate funds from paychecks. Their ability to be generous is much more a matter of stock and real property holdings, alternative investments, and old-fashioned dividends and interest. Blips on their economic radar screens should not be an impediment to the generosity of those most fortunate Americans.

In any event, the advice offered here will work in good or bad economic periods. A source of guidance for all seasons, you are invited to place the precepts of *Yours for the Asking* into practice. Ride the wave of American prosperity, or cushion the blow of occasional austerity, with this guidebook at your side.

It is estimated that there are at least 125,000 full-time professional fundraisers in America. Every one of them needs to read this book. And fully 26,000 of them are members of the Association of Fundraising

Professionals. Illustrative of the rapid growth of the fundraising profession is this striking fact. The Johns Hopkins University employs more people in its fundraising operation, 350 strong, than it has professors in its School of Arts and Sciences.

Those paid to raise funds only scratches the surface of the audience for *Yours for the Asking*. One of the principal obligations of trustees of nonprofit organizations is to donate charitable funds and to raise them, or more colloquially, to give and get. The actual number of board members in the United States is reliably estimated at 4 million.[2] But there are many other volunteers raising funds who are not trustees. Indeed, on average, adult Americans devote five hours per week of their time volunteering for a nonprofit institution or cause.[3] No small portion of those hours are given to raising funds or in kind support.

The associations of fundraisers are categorized by sector: health, education, social services, arts and culture, and the like; gender and ethnicity; geographic location: city, state, region, national; and new and emerging causes.

These organizations, numbering in the hundreds, all are devoted to improving the efficiency and effectiveness with which funds are raised. *Yours for the Asking* is intended to help them advance that objective.

The audience for this primer on fundraising is intended to extend even beyond professionals who get paid to do it, trustees who are expected to do it, and volunteers who offer to do it.

What about the politicians who are constantly in the fundraising marketplace?

Or hedge fund, private equity, and other investment professionals who prowl the world in search of capital to invest or deploy?

Or the tens of thousands of students studying at any of the hundreds of colleges and specialized institutions to prepare for careers in nonprofit institutions?

In the measure that fundraising is an act of persuasion, of winning friends and influencing people, *Yours for the Asking* can help anyone in the business of separating people from their assets or income for a purpose that serves the public.

Yours for the Asking is a guide, a manual, a how-to for all those with an instinct to raise funds and those who harbor fears or qualms about doing so.

It explains in easy-to-understand language how to reach wealthy people face to face, in writing, in large groups, at special events, and over the Internet. And once you've gained access to them and gotten their attention, how to bring home the bacon.

It helps solve the mystery of fundraising from foundations, those notoriously elusive entities that seem to house experts in closing doors, ignoring solicitations, and, when pressed for an answer, saying no.

It demonstrates how many ways there are to tap the resources of donors, large and small, for the institution or cause that commands your respect, affection, and attention.

It helps you to locate the intersection between the interests of business and the needs of your nonprofit organization. Find those connections, and you will easily tap corporate resources.

The book not only offers pithy lessons in memorable language but includes examples as exhibits. The persuasive and moving follow-up letter to a face-to-face solicitation. The compelling foundation proposal. The direct mail piece that breaks through the clutter of the mailbox. These illustrative materials help to show the reader "how to," not just offer advice from "on high."

As the president of Lincoln Center, the world's largest performing arts center, I've led in the effort to raise over $1 billion in a six-year period. As president of the International Rescue Committee, a very different organization serving not art lovers but impoverished refugees and displaced people, I've raised hundreds of millions of dollars. As the architect and founder of the AT&T Foundation in 1983 and 1984, then the largest corporate philanthropic enterprise in America, I gave away, in a dozen years, well in excess of $1 billion of support. And as executive director of the 92nd Street Y, trustee of over a dozen institutions, and volunteer to at least an equal number, I've raised hundreds of millions more.

In fact, my friends and colleagues have been heard to say that almost every call from Reynold is a collect call.

Yours for the Asking is the distillation of all that I've learned from these experiences about requesting help, soliciting support, and asking for money. It is intended to be useful to small, medium-size, and large organizations running the gamut from health to education, from the arts to humanitarian causes, from think tanks and advocacy groups to community-based outfits and social services providers, and from the established to the fledgling. Tightly woven into America's social and civic fabric are nonprofits that together are important enough to become known as America's Third Sector, business and government being the first two. For that Third Sector to thrive and with it for America to seize its opportunities and meet its challenges, philanthropic support must grow mightily.

I hope that you will benefit from my triumphs and defeats, successes and humiliations on the playing fields of twenty-first-century philanthropy.

We begin in Chapter 1 with an explanation of why I believe there is a yet-to-be-tested elasticity to charitable contributions. The staggering growth of net assets in America, and globally, spells opportunity for all those seeking to solve serious problems, to repair some part of our broken world.

Fundraising to realize such dreams should be the welcome responsibility not just of development staff, but of the president, executive director, or chief executive officer and the members of the board of directors at whose pleasure he or she serves.

The capacity to contribute at levels much, much higher than the $306 billion raised in 2007 is undeniable. The critical needs addressed by the nongovernmental organizations in America are proven and persuasive. The profound obligation to convince those with the wherewithal to give more of themselves to institutions and causes larger than themselves falls to you and your professional and lay colleagues.

That is not a burden. It is a pleasure. That is not a job. It is a calling.

What's needed is a description of how best to raise funds, particularly from individuals, who consistently represent 80 percent of all giving in

America. Chapters 2 and 3 attempt to capture the temperament and technique, the teamwork and homework, the act of acquiring an appointment, and the art of face-to-face solicitation, in writing and by phone, formally and informally.

There is not a trick up my sleeve, a clever maneuver in my mind, or a mystery that I leave undisclosed. You'll long to tear yourself away from the printed page and ask for a gift right now, right away, as in why wait?

Oddly, not nearly enough attention is paid to the members of a nonprofit board of directors as a major, indispensable fundraising source. I argue that the cultivation of trustees for major gifts falls to the president as much as anyone else. How trustees are treated, how highly they are valued in the governance process, and how much focused time is spent on tapping their intellectual gifts and business and social connections is critical to successfully raising funds from them.

Institutional donors, foundation and corporate, are a special challenge. Unlike most individuals, they often come equipped with guidelines, rules, regulations, and eligibility criteria that, taken together, are high barriers to entry. Neither entities are models of transparency or clarity. They are difficult to figure out, hard to access, and, certainly by comparison with the individual donor, slow to move.

Overcoming these obstacles is well worth the effort. To general donors, the imprimatur of foundation and corporate support is weighty. It suggests that due diligence was conducted in a highly competitive process. It not infrequently conveys multiyear support, and, in the case of corporations, may involve in-kind gifts and cash from the expense budgets of lines of business or staff departments within the firm as well as from its philanthropic arm.

Explaining how best to win funds from these two very different kinds of institutional donors is the aim of Chapter 4. It is written from the vantage point not only of a frequent solicitor, but of a former trustee and chair of a large family foundation (the Nathan Cummings Foundation) and president of a very large corporate fund (the AT&T Foundation).

As individual investors are instructed over and over again to diversify their portfolios, we are told that how we allocate assets by sector (commodities, treasuries, domestic common stock—large cap, small cap, mid-cap—foreign stock in mature economies, emerging markets, hedge funds, private equity) may be more important than the particular firms or funds we invest in.

The equivalent kind of thinking for the fundraiser begs the question of how to divide our finite resources between pursuit of the individual and institutional, on one hand, and the many techniques of fundraising on the other. In Chapter 5, I choose two fundraising methods to illuminate, special events and direct mail. The specialized skills applicable to each will become abundantly apparent, as is the connection between these ways of soliciting funds and climbing the ladder of fundraising success with any individual donor. For what special events and direct mail have in common is that they allow us to identify individuals of particular philanthropic promise who merit personal attention.

Lawyers are frequently heard to observe that an oral agreement is not worth the paper it is written on. I sometimes feel that way about fundraising. It is a field more talked about and around than practiced and more discussed than written about. So I've selected from among the very challenging questions I've been asked about the how-tos, whys, and wherefores of this still-mysterious process and taken a stab at providing what I hope are cogent answers. That's what Chapter 6 is all about.

In Chapter 7, I distill from the book pithy lessons about fundraising that you can consult regularly. They comprise my hymnal. I recite them as in a totemic incantation. They give away my most precious secrets. It is inconceivable that you will heed this advice and not experience significant improvement in your fundraising. With such a claim, I exhibit the self-confidence of a veteran fundraiser. Please forgive me.

Fundraising doesn't work unless it combines inspiration with perspiration. Motivating yourself, day in and day out, means being reminded that what we do in the vineyards of the Third Sector really matters and that donors provide the equity and the venture capital that make miracles happen—in the hospital, in the classroom, in the research laboratory, on the stage, and amid some of the most desperate conditions of failed states around the world, where dire poverty, instability, and refugees and displaced people abound.

I take the occasion to remind us that the first three letters in the word fundraising are fun. The whole endeavor is fun, actually. Lots of it. And I've been fortunate to enjoy a fair share.

Chapter 8 tells some very funny stories about my adventures in fundraising. They have only one thing in common. Every one of them is true. No exaggeration. No hyperbole. Well, almost! Humor with a point of view and some important lessons to learn.

In Chapter 9, we explore the future of fundraising, attempting to discern long-term trends, best put here in the form of questions:

What is the likelihood that philanthropy will become globalized? Will individuals and charitable funds emanating from other nations become approachable by stateside charities?

Will Internet fundraising eventually move from a relatively small niche, relevant to smaller donors and identifiable causes, to much more substantial donations and a more generic appeal?

Are private equity, hedge funds, and investment firms generally a potential source of increased giving, orders of magnitude larger than is true today?

How do nonprofit institutions need to change to prepare to capture these opportunities?

To keep you motivated, I'd urge reading the pages of Chapter 10 now and again. They contain favorite quotations on philanthropy and its results. They instruct. They elevate. They are bound to move you to action with a sense of urgency and of pride.

Finally, the book ends with recommendations on further reading. Dig deeply into the literature. Doing so will not only help to improve your skills as a fundraiser; it will help make you into a more interesting, lively, informed professional. It will incent donors to spend time with you because they are likely to benefit from who you have become and what you have learned.

CHAPTER I

FUNDRAISING: A CALL TO ALMS, A CALL TO ACTION

You must be the change you wish to see in the world.

The difference between what we do and what we are capable of doing would suffice to solve most of the world's problems.

—Mahatma Gandhi

How many activities in life are as unpopular as fundraising? Most people, often including trustees who are obligated to ask for money on behalf of the nonprofit institutions they serve, and professionals, paid to solicit funds, would rather walk slowly over hot coals.

There's something very intimidating about approaching a friend or a relative stranger and requesting a gift. It's widely viewed as a bold and presumptuous act, one filled with the potential for awkwardness, embarrassment, disappointment, and rejection.

Chief executives of hospitals, universities, and cultural institutions often cite raising money as the least pleasant and most trying of their responsibilities. Many trustees, when faced with the choice, would prefer to donate more than they would otherwise rather than solicit others.

1

The average length of stay of the presidents of large nonprofits in almost any field including higher education, arts and culture, hospitals, and social service institutions is now some seven years. An important reason for such relatively short terms of service is carrying the burden of the relentless pursuit of charitable gifts, 24/7.

A generation ago, proud and preening parents would brag about their son "the doctor" or "the lawyer." Nowadays it is the fashion to say one's children are in hedge funds or private equity. Have you ever heard a mother or father look up to the sky and say "Lord, I wish my child becomes a fundraiser!"?

Truth be told, the answer to that question is more than likely to be no.

That's a pity.

For in its broadest sense, raising funds is a business skill of the highest order. It is precisely what private equity and hedge managers do everyday to attract capital for their acquisitions and investments. It's what allows hospitals and institutions of higher education to convince the tax-exempt bond market to support their physical expansion or modernization. And it's an attribute every chief executive of every nonprofit institution needs to possess.

Put simply, fundraising is nothing more than salesmanship. It's persuasiveness at work. It's a performing art.

No parents should shy away from acknowledging that their kids have mastered this form of stagecraft.

Let me begin, then, with a confession.

I like raising money. I like everything about it.

The science of solidly grounded research. The process of solving the mystery of human motivation. The skill of asking well, face to face. Formulating a persuasive written proposal to which the reader cannot reply negatively. Organizing the well-designed, well-executed, well-received special event.

Helping a successful executive find new meaning and joy in life from a charitable gift. Assisting a corporate vice president to identify the perfect intersection, the sweet spot, where business interest and societal need intersect. Inspiring veteran trustees to do more to strengthen their institutions and recruit newcomers to the cause. Unleashing the energy that animates private acts for the public good.

How could anyone not be moved by the challenge of these activities and by the nobility of the ends they seek to realize?

Using language and images evocatively to convince and enchant. Transforming ideas and dreams into realities by eliciting that magic word, *yes*, from an individual, a foundation staffer, or a company executive.

Listening carefully to donors allows you to bring back invaluable observations to the line staff of your agency and assist in their quest for continuous improvement.

Raising funds from donors helps to create and sustain environments in which gifted professionals can do their best work.

What a thrill. What a high.

In the year 2007, $306 billion of charitable funds were raised, a new record, 3.9 percent above the prior year. This sum is 2.1 percent of America's gross domestic product. And billions more found their way to nonprofits through a dazzling variety of in-kind gifts and from marketing, sales, advertising, and human resource budgets, forms of support that go largely uncounted by such authoritative sources as *Giving USA*.

But who among us does not fail to imagine by how many orders of magnitude that figure could grow, and what such growth could mean to healing the sick, training the unemployed, educating the student, researching tomorrow's cure, maintaining our nation's competitiveness, and eliminating poverty, AIDS, malaria, tuberculosis, and starvation from the face of the earth?

The number of U.S. households with a net worth of $1 million or more rose to 8.4 million in 2006, up from 6 million in 2001. The number of households with a net worth of $5 million or more now exceeds 1 million.[1] It's not just about the title of best-selling books.[2] The millionaire next door and the middle-class millionaire are realities. And in the aggregate, Americans have been giving away to charity somewhat more than they collectively save each year.

Are we reaching to such new and expanded sources of unimaginable affluence in our midst: the beneficiaries of the commercial real estate boom, or the explosion of wealth that characterizes the private equity and hedge fund communities, for example?

Are we expanding our boards of directors and asking our trustees to give in proportion to their means and in accordance with their most generous impulses?

Are we learning adequately from the successes of others? The pluperfect benefit that sends the donor home thanking you for the opportunity; the direct mail solicitation that breaks through the clutter of busy lives to sing "We need your help" in a not-to-be-denied melody and lyric; the cultivation of leadership that takes off with powerful, peer-driven asking?

So much of the health of the institution you represent resides in how effectively you embrace its mission, harness the energy of advocates, and rally the fortunate to its cause.

Occasional setbacks in the national economy are more likely to be speed bumps than serious barriers to fundraising success. As I write, debate ensues about whether the American economy is in a recession and, if so, for how long and how deep. Short and shallow is my guess. But no matter, don't let the naysayers and skeptics, the preachers of doom and gloom slow you down, or alter your mood. The power of positive thinking is the very fuel that animates the best fundraisers and salesmen.

Just consider what could have happened to prevent or cure disease, to alleviate poverty, to expand rates of literacy and numeracy, if individual giving and bequests had grown from 2001 to 2006 not at a compound annual rate of 5.3 percent and 3 percent, respectively, but at roughly double that rate 10.5 percent, and 5.9 percent, respectively. Such improved performance would have yielded a total of $62.5 billion in philanthropy, increasing individual giving from the base year 2001 of $172.4 billion not to its real figure of $222.9 billion but to $284.6 billion. Similarly, bequests would have grown from a 2001 base year of $19.8 billion, not to the real figure of $22.9 billion but to $26.4 billion.

By only doubling the rate of growth of individual and bequest giving, contributors in America would have moved overall from $295 billion in contributions to $360 billion by 2006, for a 22 percent growth rate.

Okay, the past is gone and we cannot do anything to improve performance retroactively. Looking to the future, then, if we take the 2006 total of $295 billion and assume its compound annual growth rate is identical to prior years, we will arrive at 2011 with a total giving figure of $377.5 billion. However, if we set an achievable goal of doubling the compound rate of growth of individual and bequest giving, that total will be 22 percent larger, or $461.3 billion. Just imagine how these additional funds would help to address the pressing issues of global warming, of access to and graduation from the nation's colleges and universities, of reducing substance abuse and funding safe, proven alternatives to incarceration in this country.

To state the gap between the promise of fundraising and its performance another way, consider generosity geographically, ranked by states.[3] While California and New York enjoy the highest aggregate wealth as measured by investment assets, according to a six-year study by the New Tithing Group, a San Francisco–based think tank, these states rank twenty-first and twenty-third in terms of generosity, giving about 0.74 percent of their income to charity annually.

By contrast, affluent residents of Utah and Oklahoma donate 1.63 percent and 1.05 percent, respectively, in annual giving.

Consider this: If the top earners in the nation's five wealthiest states (California, New York, Florida, Texas, and Illinois) donated at the rate of the benefactors in the five most generous (Utah, Oklahoma, Nebraska, Minnesota, and Georgia), giving from individuals would have risen in 2005 by $13 billion.

Generosity is unevenly distributed geographically. Raising the level of giving from those states in which more wealthy people live to those in which the affluent give most generously would work wonders. Expanding where generosity lives is a terrific challenge for fundraisers and a tonic for some of the most serious problems that ail the nation and the planet.

AMERICA'S CHARITABLE POTENTIAL

Let your imagination take hold in yet another way. Jeffrey Sachs, the Columbia University economist who is leading an effort to eliminate poverty and vastly reduce mortality and morbidity in the Third World, dreams grandly:

> According to *Forbes* magazine, there are some 950 billionaires in the world, with an estimated combined wealth of $3.5 trillion. Even after all the yachts, mansions and luxury living that money can buy many times over, these billionaires will still have nearly $3.5 trillion to save the world. Suppose they pooled their wealth, as [Warren] Buffett has done with Bill and Melinda Gates. By standard principles of foundation management, a $3.5 trillion endowment would have a 5% payout of about $175 billion a year, an amount sufficient to extend basic health care to all in the poorest world; end massive pandemics of AIDS, TB and malaria; jump-start an African Green Revolution; end the digital divide; and address the crying need for safe drinking water for 1 billion people. In short, this billionaire's foundation would be enough to end extreme poverty itself.[4]

Whether by increasing the rate of growth of giving by American individuals and institutions, or by spreading generosity more evenly across state boundaries or by persuading the ultra-rich to emulate the Buffett and Gates families, what remains abundantly clear is how much room there is for improvement in our performance as fundraisers.

I write *Yours for the Asking* out of a conviction that fundraising is an important ingredient of what makes great things happen in our inventive, problem-solving nonprofit sector and out of a strong sense that we who are charged with the privilege of raising funds can do better. Much better.

America is the richest country on earth. And while the municipal, state, and federal governments have indispensable roles to play, as do socially responsible businesses, we have yet to witness anything like the full flowering of American philanthropy.

Will another generation of public school kids be deprived of the education they deserve?

Will it be said of this generation that by dint of our efforts, the beginning of the end of poverty truly occurred for the 2 billion people on earth who live on two dollars or less each day?

How soon will cures for Parkinson's disease and cancer be found?

In the chain of human improvement, those who play leadership roles in nonprofit institutions can be among the strongest links.

I urge you to go about your business with energy, determination, and pride. Much that matters depends on your performance. Many in need know not how much they rely on your skill, professionalism, and attitude.

My reference to "attitude" is no accident. My kinship with those who raise money voluntarily, or for a living, is rooted in their conviction that problems are really opportunities and that obstacles are really minor roadblocks. And my affinity with you flows from your optimism and resilience.

Prospective donors who turn us down never mean no. They mean "now is not the time," or "less," or "have someone else ask me," or "craft your case more effectively." But our cause is too important, our clients too needy, our world in too much disrepair to take no for an answer. For all of us, the word "no" must be the beginning of a conversation.

In short, the best of those who call development their obligation or their profession are strong believers in Noah's principle, which says "No more credit for predicting rain. Credit only for building arks."

Yours for the Asking is intended to be an ark-building primer, a back-to-basics, Fundraising 101 written by someone who has raised money all of his life. I have done so as a professional, principally at the 92nd Street Y, a community center of some distinction located in Manhattan; at the International Rescue Committee, one of the largest and most consequential refugee relief organizations in the world; and at Lincoln Center for the Performing Arts, the most comprehensive institution of its kind anywhere. As a trustee, I've raised funds for dozens of organizations on whose boards I served. And as a philanthropist, it has been my privilege to guide millions of dollars of gifts at the Nathan

Cummings Foundation, hundreds of millions of donations as the president of the AT&T Foundation, and well over $2 million in our family's personal giving.

I cite our family's own proclivity to give for three reasons.

First, it is virtually impossible to ask others to behave in a way contrary to your own conduct. Asking well works when the solicitor is a true believer, a missionary of sorts. The test of that conviction is more than moving prose or spirited rhetoric. You can open the mind of the prospect wider if you have opened your own wallet or pocketbook before your visit. Giving is infectious. The virus of philanthropy starts with the solicitor.

Second, my wife and I have always built donations into our annual budget. We set aside 10 percent of what we earn to benefit others. We do so out of an ardent belief in our obligation to help needy causes and people.

Read the Talmud:

> It is not required of thee to complete the task, but neither art thou free to desist therefrom. . . . He who saves one life, it is as if he has saved the whole world.

Or consult the Bible (I Corinthians):

> And now abideth faith, hope, charity, these three; but the greatest of these is charity.

Apart from religious sources of inspiration, our giving flows from our convictions and caring. It recognizes the need to discharge obligations to the boards we have been privileged to serve on. We also reserve some funds to respond affirmatively to the favorite causes of our friends, just as we would hope they will be responsive to our appeals. We wish we could do more. We hope we are modestly helpful.

Giving, then, for us and for hundreds of thousands of other Americans is not simply a matter of playing roles as professionals or trustees, nor of being proficient in foundation and corporate giving and nonprofit asking. It is very much part of our personal conduct, day in, day out. It is more than what we do. It is who we are.

As the old gospel song has it, "We are the ones we've been waiting for."

To convert this set of diverse experiences into lessons learned for others to benefit from has been a joy. I hope that you will be the better fundraiser after having digested *Yours for the Asking* and that as a result, you and your colleagues will allow tens of thousands of Americans to experience the joy of gifts to others, for the first time or in greater sum. Little could please me more. And those donors will be grateful to you, as well they should be.

Indeed, when going about fundraising for your favorite organization or cause, think boldly, creatively, and resourcefully.

Too often, professionals and volunteers are constrained by history (we've always done it this way), by labels (that individual or institution will not be interested in supporting our organization because . . .), by inertia (what is true of physics is true of fundraising; solicitors at rest tend to stay at rest, those in motion tend to remain in motion), and by risk aversion (don't go there, he or she may say no or, don't go down that alley, it may be blind).

ACTIVATING PHILANTHROPY: THE 92ND STREET Y

I recall my years as executive director of the 92nd Street Y. When I arrived there in 1977, the place did reasonably well in approaching traditional supporters of community centers and of Jewish-sponsored institutions. After all, this Y was then and remains now the oldest and largest Jewish-affiliated organization of its kind in the United States.

But the 92nd Street Y served senior adults, operated summer camps, and supported a large youth residence. It managed one of the largest health clubs in New York City; housed a very well regarded nursery school; sponsored a wide-ranging performing arts, literary, and film program and an eclectic, high-profile, diverse spoken word series; among many other activities.

Still, the staff and board by and large did not solicit funding sources interested in these specific activities, or art forms, or program formats.

Doing so would have meant multiplying very substantially the number of relationships to be cultivated, proposals to be drafted, research to be conducted, and special events to be held. It would have required trustees to look in the mirror and ask more of themselves and of one another. It would have meant raising the organization's metabolism, not to mention its sights.

GALVANIZING GIVING: THE INTERNATIONAL RESCUE COMMITTEE

Two decades later, I found myself the chief executive officer of the International Rescue Committee (IRC), a nongovernment organization that then spent about $175 million annually resettling refugees in the United States and serving refugees and displaced people abroad in over two dozen countries with health, education, community development, agricultural, job creation, and leadership training services. Here, too, I was surprised to discover that almost 60 years after its founding, the IRC focused its fundraising almost exclusively on institutions and individuals who cared about the plight of refugees and of displaced people.

But why not approach funding sources interested in Africa, Asia, and the Balkans, the regions where the IRC provided such extensive services?

How about soliciting those who care about the welfare of children and of women? After all, 80 percent of the population of refugee camps consists of kids and of females.

What about the wealthy concerned with preventing communicable disease—tuberculosis, cholera, malaria, AIDS, and the like?

The IRC recruited very bright, idealistic, resourceful, and determined Americans, Asians, Africans, and European expatriates to manage its programs and lead the thousands of national employees it retained around the world. These young adults, largely in their 20s and 30s, were very well educated, brimming with promise and possessed of many career options.

That they chose a humanitarian agency for employment and that they worked in complex, difficult, and dangerous conditions drew the admiration of many sources of wealth. Why not lead with strength and approach funding sources for staff support—salary supplements; training and educational opportunities; reward, recognition, and retention programs; recruitment drives; and the like?

The opportunities for fundraising were abundant. The gap between the IRC's fundraising promise and its performance was huge. In less than six years, annual private fundraising at the IRC quintupled, funding sources expanded by orders of magnitude, programs received much-needed annual support, and a $2 million cash reserve blossomed alongside a newly created $40 million endowment fund.

FUNDRAISING ON STEROIDS: LINCOLN CENTER

And so it was at Lincoln Center. If you were a donor conspicuous by your expressed interest in the performing arts, Lincoln Center created a positive connection with you, more likely than not. But the Lincoln Center Institute, its education arm that seeks to integrate the arts into the curriculum of elementary and secondary schools, was, by comparison, virtually a secret outside of our own walls. Funding sources committed to improvements in our public schools and intrigued by Lincoln Center as an external catalyst for positive change; those focused on the "outer boroughs" of Brooklyn, Queens, Staten Island, and the Bronx; and all those interested in community relations were also ripe to be approached. Indeed, we began to think of Lincoln Center not just as a consortium of 12 world-class and world-renowned artistic organizations but as a source of civic pride, as a huge tourist attraction, and as an engine of economic development.

Conceived in this expanded way, Lincoln Center could solicit wealthy institutions and individuals who were not necessarily drawn to, let alone passionate about, any art form. It could approach developers, retailers, and restauranteurs on the Upper West Side of Manhattan, all of whom benefit inordinately from the 5 million visitors who each year enjoy Lincoln Center's performances, its school activities, its free programs, its performing arts library, and its 16 acres of precious public space.

No one who owned or operated a substantial business, residence, or commercial property within 10 or 15 minutes commuting distance from Lincoln Center denied or gainsaid its beneficial financial impact. But at 45 years of age, Lincoln Center had still not systematically solicited them for donations. Now, as we fast approach our fiftieth anniversary in May 2009, we have given birth to a Lincoln Center Conservancy, a strong consortium of institutional neighbors who have pledged so far to provide a total of about $1 million annually to help maintain the handsomely redeveloped private and public facilities that have been built over the last three years. We have, in effect, created a $20 million endowment for campus maintenance, from nowhere. There is more to come, I'm confident.

Thought of in this similarly capacious way, Lincoln Center could ask itself how best to go after the hedge fund community, the private equity manager, and the successful property owners and real estate developers of New York City. These sources of support tend to regard Lincoln Center as much a civic as an artistic institution. Indeed, some value this performing arts mecca more for its contribution to the quality of life in New York City than for its advancement of music, dance, opera, theater, or film. Lincoln Center is one of those places attractive enough to draw people to live, work, and travel to Manhattan in very large numbers.

Lincoln Center's Juilliard School and School of American Ballet admit students from around the country and around the world. Their graduates are reputed to comprise as many as 30 percent of the musicians of America's leading orchestras and dancers in America's best-known ballet companies. Lincoln Center's national and global reach also manifests itself in the tours of its resident artistic organizations—the New York Philharmonic, Jazz at Lincoln Center, the New York

City Ballet and the Juilliard Orchestra—around the country and around the world. And for 31 years, Lincoln Center has raised the funds for and produced the award winning show broadcast nationally on public television called *Live From Lincoln Center*, hosted for years by Beverly Sills, until her untimely death in 2007. With television and radio audiences approaching those of *The Sopranos* and of *Sex and the City*, Lincoln Center's powerful brand can be legitimately viewed as national, not just regional or local.

Perhaps 80 percent of those who patronize Lincoln Center live in New York, Connecticut, or New Jersey. We estimate that the other 20 percent of our 5 million customers are American or overseas tourists. And through the works we commission that are performed all around the world or productions we mount that are subsequently presented elsewhere, Lincoln Center's reach is extended still further.

Under such circumstances, for fundraising purposes, we had to conceive of Lincoln Center as a national, even an international, institution. Doing so meant persuading the board of directors to invite individuals to serve as trustees whose principal residence was not in the tri-state area or whose company headquarters were located far from Manhattan, overland or overseas. It meant reaching to institutional funding sources that ordinarily do not support organizations outside of their home territory. Why shouldn't Lincoln Center be the exception that proved the rule? And it meant establishing a national and international patrons' council of arts benefactors and activists who would come to Lincoln Center, benefiting from privileged access to the best available tickets and from opportunities to attend galas and other special events throughout the year.

What is true of relatively untapped *sources* of funding for the Y, the IRC, and Lincoln Center was also the case for relatively unexploited *methods* of fundraising.

At the Y, foundations, corporations, government, and individual donors all needed attention. So, too, did proposal writing, public and community relations, benefits and galas, and major gift cultivation.

At the IRC, an across-the-board modernization and overhaul in energetically approaching all of these sources and using all of these methods were also the order of the day. In the case of this high-performing but little-known humanitarian organization, an invigorated direct mail and online fundraising drive was also high on the agenda.

For Lincoln Center, the plan to address all of these sources and apply all of these methods had to be upgraded and expanded. Otherwise, we might have jeopardized Lincoln Center's highest-quality performing arts, educational, and public service programs. The powers that be had other objectives in mind as well.

Lincoln Center needed to take the lead in the physical renovation of a 16-acre campus that would be celebrating its fiftieth anniversary in May 2009. The comprehensive public space and artistic facility modernization necessitated a capital fundraising campaign of $803 million. In addition, no one at Lincoln Center could remember when the organization last conducted an endowment campaign. To strengthen its balance sheet, we set a target of $75 million, for a total campaign goal of $878 million.

As I write, the year-over-year improvements in annual fundraising are very gratifying, growing at a compound annual rate of 10.2 percent, from $29.8 million in 2002 to $55.3 million in 2008. On the capital side, some $600 million of our $878 million goal has been raised, close to $40 million of which is thus far destined for endowment enhancement.

Appendix I contains two exhibits that portray fundraising progress and growth fueled by an enthusiastic cadre of trustees, by a set of consensus-blessed objectives, and by a Lincoln Center viewed not only as a critical artistic institution but as a civic cause, a major contributor to the quality of life in New York City, an important tourist attraction, and an engine of economic development.

Now, these examples might not be useful to every reader. Smaller, younger, less well-known organizations might not find the particular reform activities illustratively chosen for the 92nd Street Y, the IRC, or Lincoln Center applicable to their own situational settings.

A CALL TO ALMS, A CALL TO ACTION

Consider this general challenge, however.

How many institutions or causes do you know that cannot expand the cadre of trustees and volunteers that support them?

How many are insufficiently tapping their geographic, ethnic, and community-based neighbors for support?

How many are asking current supporters systematically for the names of their like-minded friends, colleagues, and associates?

Just as the nation's colleges and universities have expanded many times over the methods by which they mobilize graduates, parents, students, and faculty to enrich their coffers, and just as hospitals have avidly pursued grateful patients, so too can other nonprofits dig more deeply into their history, their Rolodexes, and their thematic and programmatic appeal to attract new and enlarged constituencies of donors.

Imagine what supplemental resources could do for your organization, its clients, and its employees.

Imagine how much more quickly or uncompromisingly its vision could be realized with more funds at your disposal.

Imagine. Then act. You can change the world for the better. To borrow from presidential candidate Barack Obama's moving incantation, "Yes, you can."

CHAPTER 2

SOLICITING INDIVIDUAL PROSPECTS

The life of money-making is one undertaken under compulsion, and wealth is evidently not the good we are seeking, for it is merely useful for the sake of something else.

—Aristotle, *Nicomachean Ethics*

He who dies rich, dies disgraced.

—Andrew Carnegie

While developing a diversified portfolio of donors is a vital sign of a healthy contributed income program, for the vast majority of nonprofits, at the epicenter of such a portfolio must be the individual donor.

When unemployment is low and wages and capital gains are healthy, giving to charity tends to be robust. Private foundation payouts rise with buoyant stock market returns. As corporate earnings improve, so does corporate philanthropy. Government support is almost always healthy when tax collections are steady or increasing. By attending to all categories of individual and institutional funding, a nonprofit benefits fully from an upbeat economy. It also cushions itself against an adverse trend affecting one or more of these sources of giving.

Too great a dependence on any one source within or between these large categories puts your operating budget at risk. Balance and a sense of proportion are the order of the day.

Nonetheless, of the $306 billion given away to charity in 2007, over 80 percent derived from individuals through live or testamentary gifts. If your organization has mastered how best to approach people for donations, then it is highly unlikely that it will fail to do as well with the other two leading sources of private funds, foundations and corporations. The processes of accessing individual donors; researching their backgrounds; identifying common ground between them and your cause; and delivering an effective presentation, face to face and in writing, differ only in degree and not in kind from succeeding with institutional sources of funds.

Develop a thoughtful, disciplined, creative approach to soliciting individuals, where most of contributed income originates year after year, and you have come a long way to preparing for good fortune with business firms and foundations.

When your fundraising program is really humming, it resembles both a ladder and the seasons of a human life.

It resembles a ladder, because ideally individual and institutional sources find donations habit forming and their relationship to your organization or cause strengthens over time. Direct mail donors become gala supporters who blossom into major givers and benefactors of a capital campaign and then offer bequests or their offspring's philanthropy to the cause. Modest corporate donations evolve into major corporate sponsorships and, ultimately, into mutually beneficial partnerships that mature over time. And so it should be with foundations and all levels of government.

Kenneth N. Dayton, the former chairman and chief executive of Dayton Hudson Corporation, describes the stages of giving for himself and his wife in this way:

1. Minimal response

2. Involvement and interest

3. As much as possible

4. Maximum allowable

5. Beyond the max

6. Percentage of wealth

7. Capping wealth

8. Reducing the cap

9. Bequests

Each phase is associated with the passing of the years, leaving more time and more wealth for philanthropic endeavors. In addition, Ken Dayton was a founder of the 5% Club in Minneapolis-Saint Paul, a group of companies pledged to give at least that percentage of their pretax net income to charity in good years and bad. Mr. Dayton was extraordinarily generous, both as a businessman and civic leader and in his private life.[1]

In fact, it is never too early to introduce newcomers to the idea of philanthropy, the sheer pleasure of helping others. Acts of giving ripen over the years and find expression in myriad gifts of time and treasure. Indeed, the children of generous parents are themselves serious candidates for excellence in ladder climbing.

At the center of a vibrant philanthropic program that pays careful attention to both fundraising targets and methods is the individual American. He or she has money to spare for charitable purposes. Go, ask for it.

AMERICA'S ASTONISHING AFFLUENCE

Although the fortunes of the American economy may fluctuate, the clear trend lines of improved productivity, of globalization, of low

unemployment, of moderate inflation, and of healthy corporate earnings are all positive. The staggering increases in the net wealth of many
Americans, the growth in the income of many others, and the felt need
to contribute to resolving society's problems and to be recognized for it
are all alive and well in America.

Offered next are diverse indicators of the "surplus capital" being
generated in this country. Taken together, the growth in American
affluence is staggering. A healthy share of it is yours for the asking.

- In 1992 when President Clinton was inaugurated, the Dow Jones
  Industrial Average stood at 3696, the Nasdaq at 586, and the
  Standard & Poor's Industrial Average at 480. As I write, those
  averages have moved to 13,625 and 2,706 and 1,504, respectively.
  Those increases, close to a quadrupling of the Dow Jones, a four-
  and-a-half times increase in the Nasdaq, and a three and a half
  times rise in the S&P, not to mention the growth in foreign stock
  exchanges or foreign currencies or commodities, spell staggering
  increases in the wealth of Americans. While arguably the working-
  class and middle-class families still struggle to maintain their
  standard of living, elsewhere unprecedented levels of affluence
  abound.

- Assets of the nation's target donor-advised funds reached $19.2
  billion in 2006, up more than 21 percent from $15.9 billion the year
  before, according to a survey of the *Chronicle of Philanthropy*.[2] In
  2006 alone, donors contributed $6 billion to their donor-advised
  funds, an increase of 25 percent from the $4.8 billion of the year
  before, well ahead of the 3.2 percent inflation rate. Further, notes
  the *Chronicle*:

  > As donors put more money into the funds, they also increased
  > the amount they gave to charities collectively. The total value
  > from donor-advised funds was $3.5 billion in 2006, a jump of
  > 18% from $3 billion in 2005. While the payout of foundation
  > assets to charity is less than 5%, donor advised funds awarded
  > a median of 17% of their assets.

- According to the eleventh annual *World Wealth Report* published by Merrill Lynch and Co. and Capgemini Group in 2006, the U.S. population of high-net-worth individuals (defined as those with at least $1 million in investible assets, excluding their primary residence) rose 9.4 percent to 2.92 million in 2004. In 2005, the same population increased 6.8 percent to 2.67 million.[3]

- In a somewhat more relaxed definition, the number of U.S. households with a net worth of more than $1 million rose to 9 million in 2008, up from 6 million in 2001, and for the first time, the number of households with a net worth of $5 million or more exceeded 1 million.[4]

- The number of ultra-high-net-worth individuals cited by *World Wealth Report*—those with at least $30 million in investible assets— increased by 11.3 percent to 94,970 in 2006.

- The *World Wealth Report* also projects that the wealth of high-net-worth individuals will reach $51.6 trillion by 2011, assuming an annual average growth rate of 6.8 percent.

- It is estimated that 1,000 people employed by Google alone each possess more than $5 million worth of the company's shares from stock grants and stock options.[5]

- It is reliably reported that more than 500,000 Americans are deca-millionaires and 463 have reached billionaire status.[6]

- In 2004, the number of hedge funds operating in America exceeded the number of mutual funds.

- In 2005, hedge fund managers earned a median of $2.05 million, an increase of 33 percent from 2004. Today, there are 9,200 hedge funds, compared to 610 in 1990. They hold $1.5 trillion of assets. According to a *McKinsey Global Institute Report* of October 2007, if you include leverage used by the hedge funds to boost returns, they own as much as $6 trillion in assets, a figure that will double by 2012.[7]

- In 2006, 26 hedge fund managers earned $130 million or more. In 2007, the best-compensated 50 hedge fund managers earned an astounding total of $29 billion.[8]

- Private equity assets under management have increased two and a half times since 2000, topping $700 billion at the end of 2006.[9]

- In 2006, Warren E. Buffett made philanthropic history by pledging $43.5 billion to the Bill and Melinda Gates Foundation and to the foundation of his wife, Susan, and his children, Howard and Susan.

- On a single evening in New York City—May 2, 2007—the Robin Hood Foundation, devoted to relieving poverty and to the improvement of primary and secondary school education, raised $72 million.

It is one thing to cite such aggregate data and anecdotal illustrations of increased wealth in America. What Claude Rosenberg, Jr. in *Wealthy and Wise*[10] demonstrates beyond a shadow of a doubt is that the affluent can comfortably double, triple, even quadruple the sums they now give to charity without depriving themselves, their families, or their heirs of any significant monetary sum or causing themselves any adverse change in lifestyle. For those in the top tax brackets, philanthropy has never been more affordable. Rosenberg argues that any concerns on this score can be fully addressed through sound investing, prudent tax planning, adequate insurance taken out on life and property, and other sound financial arrangements.

Putting surplus wealth to work is not only financially possible, it can offer a greater sense of self-esteem, a source of family purpose and solidarity, a view of money as a means to achieving ends beyond self, and a reduction of the sense of isolation from society at large that the affluent often experience. Philanthropy is an exhilarating form of self-realization. If they are properly approached, growing numbers of the wealthy will choose to move from the pursuit of private success to social consequence.

Crafting a major gift program to capture your institution's fair share of the growing philanthropic capacity in America is a major challenge and opportunity. Truly, the unrealized potential to secure more and larger gifts is simply staggering. Attention is now turned to how best to extract a greater portion of the wealth that surrounds you to benefit the commonweal.

It all begins with a generous, committed, resourceful and energetic board of directors.

TRUSTEE ENGAGEMENT AND SUPPORT

Very few nonprofits can realize fundraising success without a driven, determined group of true believers, otherwise known as trustees. If they are well selected, deeply involved, and highly motivated, then giving generously and getting assiduously becomes habit forming for them, and part of the institutional culture. Show me a nonprofit staff that drives fundraising and does not fully engage the board of directors, and I will show you an institution or cause suffering a severe case of unrealized potential.

To identify a trustee's key skills, interests, resources, and connections and to link trustees early, often, and meaningfully to the advancement of your institution's mission is hard work. It requires that you spend personal time with members of the board. This is rarely, if ever, a delegable task. At the International Rescue Committee (IRC), it even meant taking trustees along on one- or two- week trips to some very rough territory in Bosnia, Serbia, Rwanda, Eastern Congo, and East Timor, among other failed states and sites of severely displaced, desperate people. Having experienced what Frantz Fanon called the wretched of the earth in his book by that title,[11] members of the IRC board and other fellow travelers were changed forever. Loyalty to the refugee cause was now imprinted onto their consciousness.

At Lincoln Center and the 92nd Street Y, establishing firm and enduring relationships with trustees often occurred over meals or at their workplaces. In essence, we were joining forces to move a common cause to a new and better place outside the formal confines of the board room.

Of course, creating a vital committee structure to oversee the operations of a nonprofit is utterly necessary. If the meetings of your finance, audit, program, development, public relations, nominating, and executive committees are well planned and your members are well informed, creative sparks can fly at such sessions and trustees can bond to each other and to the institution. But as good as the formal apparatus may be, it is not enough. Gathering trustees with expertise to help solve specific problems or tackle detailed challenges in task forces or commissions rather than in standing committees releases energy often untapped by formal organizational structures. At Lincoln Center, we organize problem-solving groups around the application of twenty-first-century technology to our work, around the selection of a new restauranteur and caterer and a whole new approach to dining and food service generally, around the terms and conditions of seeking bond issuance to help finance our capital redevelopment program, and around planning for a multifaceted celebration of our fiftieth anniversary, to name but a few juicy challenges.

Such proliferating volunteer teams not only tap the imagination of trustee members, but often serve as constructive channels through which cash and in-kind resources of their colleagues and associates can flow.

Because the board of directors can be a powerful source of networking, of civic and political influence, of problem solving, and of generosity, I have always favored developing and working with large groups of trustees.

At the 92nd Street Y, there were 65. At the International Rescue Committee, 80. At Lincoln Center, 44 when I arrived, 68 today. This size permits one to seek diversity geographically, ethnically, occupationally, and in terms of age, gender, and point of view. It permits one to raise the financial expectations for trustees, how much each is expected to give financially or to raise each year without offending board veterans who signed up with a different understanding in mind. Resources permitting, the rising tide of generosity, of classes of well-selected newcomers filled with energy, purposefulness, and charitable funds to spare tends to lift the giving patterns of others. In philanthropy, the power of the positive example, properly displayed, is impressive. Over time, it moves others to emulate a higher standard of performance.

To be sure, there are traditionalists who argue that boards which number more than say, two dozen cannot, by definition, engage the energy and interests of its participants. My experience suggests otherwise. If the chief executive and board chair view directors not just as serving governance functions but as the vital center of a network that exerts influence, gathers intelligence, and devotes resources to the cause, then engagement of a large group of fully invested trustees is not only desirable, it is achievable.

To protect against budget cuts from local, state, and city sources of funding, to help absorb the negative impact of recession, inflation, or other economic danger signals, to cultivate new leadership, and to continually broaden the base of institutional support, it is hard to dispute the virtues of a large board of directors.

> . . . many boards of major cultural New York non-profit institutions expanded in size during the 1970's and 1980's. Although boards may also expand to diversify in other respects, one purpose of a large board is that it serves as an important fundraising tool.
>
> The New York Public Library increased its maximum board size from twenty-five to thirty-five in the mid-1970's, and then to forty two during the mid-1980's. Carnegie Hall, the New York City Ballet and the Metropolitan Opera all enlarged their boards as well.
>
> Carnegie Hall went from twenty-eight board members in the early 1970's to forty-two by the early 1980's, and forty-seven by the early 1990's. The New York City Ballet board grew from twenty-six members in the early 1980s to thirty six by the early 1990's. The Metropolitan Opera reorganized its board into various subcategories increasing its overall board size from forty-four in the early 1970's to seventy eight by the early 1990's and eighty two in the mid-1990's.[12]

In sampling a variety of distinguished arts institutions, universities, and hospitals, it was discovered that large boards have become the rule rather than the exception. The list in Appendix II of institutional board size as of 2007 often includes trustees emeriti, honorary trustees, and ex-officio trustees. But even taking those categories into account, in virtually no case has there been anything but significant growth of active, voting members of these governing boards. In many cases, the expansion has at least doubled the size of the board over a decade or less.[13]

Lincoln Center's board expansion has been quite characteristic of what has happened with virtually all of the other resident organizations on our 16-acre campus. Appendix II also lists the latest numbers for 2007, exclusive of director's emeriti, founders, and those enjoying ex-officio status.[14]

If you are wondering about the animating source of Lincoln Center's major influence, look no further than the total of 572 who are trustees of its 12 member organizations. As directors of Lincoln Center and its artistic constituents, they give freely of their own time, talent, and treasure and tap their extraordinary social and business networks on our behalf. The results are impressive and far reaching.

Still, while the trustee bodies of these organizations may be the envy of many for the business, media, investment, legal, and entrepreneurial talent they comprise, there is room for improvement. Individually and collectively, we would welcome more representation of the pharmaceutical industry, of fashion and cosmetics, of publishing, of high technology, and of the hedge fund, private equity, and venture capital communities. We would like to see more trustees whose principal residence is elsewhere around the country and around the world. And we are always on the lookout for more Latino, Asian, and African American talent.

There is a direct correlation between our fundraising success and our track record in successfully recruiting, engaging, and motivating a larger number of energetic, devoted, turned-on trustees.

The principal reason for that relationship is our clarity of expectation for trustees of Lincoln Center, in terms both of financial contribution and of service. Regarding the latter, we aspire to have every trustee attend as many meetings as possible, serve on at least one committee, and share responsibility for a project that is at the intersection of his or her knowledge and interest and Lincoln Center's needs.

As president of Lincoln Center, I view the involvement of trustees in the life of the institution as critically important.

Institutions renowned for high quality can become stodgy and complacent. John Gardner, the president of the Carnegie Corporation and founder of both Common Cause and the Independent Sector, believed strongly that these twin maladies were the greatest danger to established organizations.[15] Properly informed, inquisitive, and engaged board members pose questions and offer ideas that keep management alert to new needs, challenges, and possibilities. They combat intellectual laziness and institutional inertia.

Naturally, on a large nonprofit board, most of the work is addressed in committees, no less so than is the case in Congress. At our last board meeting of 2007, I showed the board the list of committees they had empowered, the number of meetings each had held over the preceding 12 months, and the names of the chairs of each. That chart can be found in Appendix III of this book.

The high level of discourse that occurs inside these well-staffed groups and the degree to which trustees are engaged in crafting Lincoln Center's agenda for the future are impressive. Indeed, on this list alone, 26 trustees are assuming leadership responsibilities as committee or task force chairs.

In addition, our chairman has created a kitchen cabinet of five vice-chairs who offer him advice on request. Many regard these people as potential successors to the chairman.

But committee activity is only a part of trustee engagement in Lincoln Center's work.

For example, every one of our gala events involves trustee leadership. Every time we launch a new initiative, trustees are asked to provide advice and analysis, often drawn from inside their firms, about its wisdom and direction.

Not only does the financial contribution of trustees rise with greater investment of time and energy, but the intellectual and social capital created by volunteer effort strengthens Lincoln Center in many ways. For every trustee, we aspire to have Lincoln Center be one of the three most important connections in their lives, after family and profession. I am not satisfied with anything less.

At Lincoln Center, three of our most recently elected trustees, John Hess, the chairman of Hess Oil Company, Jeff Kindler, the chairman and CEO of Pfizer, and Robert Essner, the former CEO of Wyeth, were selected on their own considerable merits but also because they fill holes in our board composition. To now enjoy the leader of one of the world's most important natural resource companies and two heads of pharmaceutical firms, an industry not noted for support of the arts anywhere outside of New Jersey, where most are headquartered, holds promise of expanding support from other corporations in these fields.

As to financial support, starting with my first board meeting, it was agreed that, with rare exceptions, we would ask new trustees to contribute personally, or acquire from their firms or elsewhere, $250,000 annually. In addition, we alerted new recruits that within a year or so, they would be approached for a seven-figure gift to our capital campaign, payable over three to five years.

In 2007, almost 30 directors contributed annually to Lincoln Center at this prescribed level, one of the most demanding of any nonprofit in the country. And while veteran trustees were attracted to the board with a different understanding, their annual giving has risen over 50 percent since the new norm was established. In addition, every trustee without exception has pledged a substantial gift to the capital campaign.

Many nonprofit boards shy away from being clear about the financial expectation for trustees or keep the price tag low to accommodate incumbent trustees who cannot or will not meet it. This is a terrible mistake. It works an injustice to those served by the nonprofit. When a board sets a higher standard and raises the sights for new trustees even without imposing the same requirement retroactively on others, its giving standards begin to change and the definition of generosity is adjusted upward. And if such a change is combined with significant board expansion, the alteration in the culture of the board and the financial results for the institution improve markedly and very swiftly.

To be sure, such change does not come without dissent, even, at times, controversy. But if there is a gap between institutional promise and performance that all agree to bridge, one of the principal means to do so is to increase the productivity and generosity of an enlarged board of directors.

Civic service at the board level is not a natural right. It is a privilege. And those who can afford to donate at far higher levels should be asked to do so.

In the harshest of terms, this point of view is sometimes known as "Give. Get. Or get off." A board that is clear about its financial and service expectation, but flexible in how it applies a new standard, recognizing that there are many ways to contribute, is a leadership group properly discharging its fiduciary and governance responsibilities.

The ambitiousness of Lincoln Center's aspirations also means we should recruit volunteers well beyond those who serve on the board.

VOLUNTEER SERVICE: BEYOND THE BOARD

Two examples will serve to demonstrate how seriously we take the opportunity for volunteer service.

First, we have created at Lincoln Center a "Counsel's Council." Chaired by the trustee head of Lincoln Center's Legal Committee and activated by the organization's extraordinary General Counsel, its members include the senior partners of some 20 of New York City's leading law firms. They have all committed their organizations to pro bono service by utilizing their associates to execute needed legal projects for which Lincoln Center would otherwise pay or, finding the cost too high, forgo.

In the year 2007, over two dozen such projects were completed, offering management guidance in how best to advance an operational matter or take a strategic initiative. We estimate the dollar value of such service to exceed $1.25 million, and we do not know of another non-profit institution in New York City with such an extensive network of pro bono legal support.

The associates of participating law firms are passionate about applying their legal skills to a public service institution like Lincoln Center and learning a great deal as they work together. Clients within Lincoln Center benefit greatly from the work product. And the senior partner members of the Counsel's Council are finding that as associates rate their Lincoln Center pro bono experience, they grant much credit to their employers for encouraging this kind of civic engagement.

Another form of the use of volunteers emanates from Lincoln Center's relationship with the Harvard Business School (HBS). Annually we recruit three or four students between their first and second year of school. They form an in-house summer consulting team whose leader is an HBS fellow, a graduate selected and hired by Lincoln Center from a pool of highly qualified applicants. The first-year salary of the fellow is split 50/50 with Lincoln Center and HBS each paying a half share. The summer interns are paid a modest honorarium.

The intellectual output of their summer term of service is very impressive. The interns have worked in areas that encompass marketing, sales, finance, development, new ventures, capital campaigns, and construction planning. Because the projects are well defined in advance of their arrival, because their internal senior staff clients look forward to these engagements, because we carefully select whom we offer intern assignments in a highly competitive process, and because I am actively involved in reviewing their work, all concerned judge this arrangement a success.

Importantly, even after these interns and fellows leave Lincoln Center's employment, most are too smitten with the institution ever to forget us. Now, in the seventh year of my tenure, there are some two dozen alumni who find themselves in important posts throughout corporate America, the Third Sector, and government. We continue to call upon their volunteer services early and often. We are never turned down.

ENGAGING VOLUNTEERS: A MANAGEMENT PRIORITY

It is important to acknowledge that many, perhaps even most, CEOs find it difficult to work with boards, volunteers, and employees in an open, participatory way. Their decision-making process is not widely shared but closely held. Their model is hierarchical and vertical, not horizontal and open.

My view and temperament are entirely different. Engaging the energy of a large board of directors demands a willingness to provide its members with vital information, to seek and listen to their points of view, and to endeavor to form an active, forward-looking consensus. Part of the fun of being a chief executive is learning from others who have accomplished much in their chosen professions and who join in the common objective of strengthening Lincoln Center. Their experiences and knowledge enrich my own and become part of the collective judgment that determines the direction of a major civic enterprise.

I am reminded of the remark of a beloved figure in New York City affairs named Henry Stern who served as Commissioner of Parks in the administrations of both Mayors Koch and Giuliani. Before then, he was elected as a city councilman. One day on the floor of the council's chambers, he railed away against those who would accuse the New York City Council of being a rubber stamp. Stern is reputed to have uttered these words:

> No one can legitimately claim that this body is a rubber stamp. Ladies and gentlemen, a rubber stamp leaves as impression. And this is something the New York City Council has never done.

Well, the chief executive officers of nonprofits serve at the pleasure of their boards, and they are not likely to perform much more ably than the quality of the staff they lead. Both board and staff join in a form of public service called a nonprofit enterprise, and both do so because they harbor the desire to make a difference, to leave an impression.

Inviting the opinions of trustees and employees, seeking to learn from those around you is untidy. It takes time and patience. If one is not careful, doing so runs the risk of slow decision making, of lowest-common-denominator groupthink, even of paralysis. This I would not permit. But the benefits of acknowledging that a place like Lincoln Center is a public trust that needs to respect the views of trustees and staff, donors and journalists, ticket buyers and passersby are simply incalculable.

Indeed, in thinking about trustees as donors to be cultivated, as bosses whose role merits respect, and as informed although sometimes critical loyalists, I have come to conclude that enriching the governance of Lincoln Center is a prominent objective for not just the chairman but for the president. In the board resides the intelligent memory of the institution. It is the affluence and far-reaching influence of its members that can allow Lincoln Center to bridge the gap between its enormous promise and its gratifying performance. And it is the board that sets the strategic course of the institution and determines whether the president is the best professional to lead its members and its professional staff.

To underutilize or undervalue this resource called a board of directors is a frequent cause not only of fundraising disappointment but of institutional drift, if not failure.

This point of view about the paramount importance of the board pervades the way I function as Lincoln Center's president.

I spend a great deal of time with trustees, not only in committee meetings, but one on one. I take it as a personal responsibility to have new members of the board feel welcome and longer-term trustees not feel taken for granted. This means lots of correspondence, of phone calls, of sharing favorite books, ideas, and tips as to what's worth seeing in the performing arts, not just around New York City but around the country and around the world.

I try to see every trustee alone for breakfast, lunch, or dinner each year or, alternatively, to entertain directors, their spouses, and other guests before and during concerts, operas, ballets, chamber music performances, solo recitals, modern dance, film, theater, and the like.

I remind myself all of the time about how individual participants must see the pleasures and benefits of board service. Some seek recognition among their peers. Others love to be in on the social activity, to see or be seen. Many enjoy being associated with an important cause, a major civic institution, and to be able to state that because of their service, Lincoln Center is stronger now than it was before they signed on. Some find being on the board a useful contribution to advancing their business interests. After all, board colleagues are sources of vital information and potential clients, partners, and investors. Others are involved because their spouse really wants them to be, or because their company CEO believes Mr. or Mrs. So and So should represent the firm on Lincoln Center's board.

Whatever the motivation, most trustees have certain characteristics in common. They enjoy learning. They treasure meaningful involvement in the vital activities of Lincoln Center. They believe that engagement with it should be fun. Everyone has enough tension and pressure at their own workplaces or in their own families. They do not volunteer to be gluttons for any such punishment in civic life. More than anything else, trustees wish to be respected for who they are and for what they can offer.

It is my job to figure that out and take the lead in wish fulfillment.

A CEO'S MODUS OPERANDI

My operating style is simple: Answer every phone call, every email, and every piece of correspondence on the day it is received, not just from trustees, but from everyone.

Take meetings seriously. Prepare for them diligently. Start and end on time. Present enough information and data to create a context that elicits participation from trustees, but not so much as to have them feel like stage props present at a ritual that could go on just as well without them.

Involve key staff at board sessions. Trustees are interested in who does what at Lincoln Center. They enjoy being exposed to younger staff whose enthusiasm and daring more than compensate for their lack of polish and occasional awkwardness or indiscretion.

But include only those employees who are related to the agenda. Board meetings where too many staff are present make trustees feel as if they are in a fish bowl being observed. Too many staff exerts a chilling effect on honest, uninhibited candor, precisely what you should be aiming to evoke from your trustees.

Information is widely shared, not closely held. Employees are encouraged to interact with trustees outside of formal settings. They become part of the social glue, the informal ties that bind an organization into a cohesive, productive whole.

The best meetings involve trustees presenting items on which they have worked and about which they are passionate. Staff members are present to support such remarks and to respond to more detailed questions that might arise. Helping my staff colleagues to distinguish between policy and operations, between the board's role and their own, and exploring why they might not be needed at any given session is a challenge. But the result—energetic, purposeful, engaged meetings—makes all of the effort worthwhile.

For meeting protagonists, there are explicit thank-yous on the spot or by email/letter on the day. For those who could not be present, a comprehensive meeting summary is sent out immediately after the meeting, almost always with a personal, handwritten postscript, telling trustees how much they were missed or conveying a message about the agenda.

It was the director Mike Nichols, who, in referring to comedy, allowed as how a laugh is a "yes". Whenever we can convey information in an amusing way that captures attention, why not? One can place a Mostly Mozart Festival brochure in a board information package, or one can ask a staff member to dress head to toe as Mr. Mozart, complete with powdered wig, and ask her to hand brochures to delighted trustees as they come off the elevator on the way to a meeting.

One can announce that we have reached a critical milestone in our capital campaign of $500 million in pledges of support, or we can place at the seat of every trustee custom messages on M&Ms that mark the occasion. We can talk about the news media coverage or public service advertisements about Lincoln Center and its constituents, or we can show samples on wide screens in the boardroom.

If the president and chair lead in taking the work of Lincoln Center more seriously than we take ourselves, if we can employ self-deprecating humor, if we combine sound preparation of important subjects with civilized discourse about them, our colleagues feel good about themselves.

The extraordinary record of meeting attendance and the wide range of trustee participation in the far-flung endeavors of Lincoln Center suggest that we must be on to something.

As a result, Lincoln Center's board members are active fundraisers. Assisted by development staff, they invite prospects to Green Room dinners, solicit table commitments to galas, open doors of friends and colleagues to solicitation calls, and introduce staff to potential sources of support in corporations, small businesses, professional firms, and foundations.

When a close customer, client friend, or colleague calls, potential donors pick up the phone.

When they write, the recipient reads.

When help is requested, it is rarely refused.

In the struggle to raise funds, even beyond their own personal and institutional generosity, there is no ally more valuable than your trustees.

Treat them accordingly, for that reason, among many others.

ATTITUDE AND TEMPERAMENT

Fundraisers must be self-confident, upbeat, optimistic, poised professionals.

No one likes to give money to the "furrowed brow" or the institution or cause in trouble. Everyone enjoys a smile and that sense of optimism that comes from associating with a winner.

Fundraisers like people. Their social energy is infectious. They keep in frequent touch with donors and prospects. They understand that the worst time to show up or to ask for help is when you want something.

Rather, raising substantial funds is the result of forming a solid relationship with a prospect. When people with means wake up each morning, they do not think of themselves, first and foremost, as donors. They naturally resist being treated that way. Rather, they are parents, grandparents, professionals, and citizens.

Affluent people, more often than not, are brimming over with ideas, questions, and opinions about the organization or cause you represent. It pays to listen carefully, to benefit from their experience, to learn what is behind their point of view. Doing so conveys respect.

Existing and potential donors are frequently sources of excellent advice and guidance. Many rich people achieve their success by keeping well informed and alert; by being curious and by asking probing, even impertinent questions. The same observation applies to the chief executives of foundations and the dispensers of corporate philanthropy.

A great risk even to prominent institutions is that they become self-satisfied and insular. The forces at work to reduce that risk are few: a discerning and responsible board of trustees; probing journalists; some form of meaningful peer review; an internal performance report card; and existing or potential donors.

Treat the latter as stakeholders in your future and as sources of guidance. Engage in empathic listening and respectful dialogue. Express interest in the personal and professional life of your prospect. This is the formula for acquiring enduring support and sustaining a genuine partnership.

If you ask for money prematurely without understanding and involving the prospect meaningfully, then empty advice, if not a quick brush-off, is the likely outcome.

Wealthy people have more to give an institution or cause than "merely" money. Typically, they harbor ideas, points of view, opinions, and questions that are often valuable. Precisely because their perspective is uncluttered by too many facts, they frequently can see more clearly than those inside of the organization, not least its chief executive.

By asking for advice and by listening carefully to it, you are showing deference to your prospect and treating him or her as a source of counsel, not just of cash. The process of engagement in the life of the institution or cause begins with open conversation. Sometimes the partner in your dialogue has it all wrong and starts off on a very critical note, unfairly so. Thick skin and patience are required. More often than not, your prospect is prepared to learn, particularly if you are genuinely interested in what he or she has to say.

One of the most telling criticisms of Secretary of State Colin Powell during the first term of George W. Bush's administration is how little he traveled, how few face-to-face visits he had with our allies and our adversaries in their neighborhoods. Pro forma photo ops and perfunctory meetings in Washington are no substitute for coming to know leading statesmen and their situational settings on the ground, in their home countries.

The unintended consequence of this standoffishness, this docility, this lack of curiosity and sheer effort was to have America seen as indifferent to the views of others, if not arrogant.

In diplomacy as in fundraising, to achieve your objective, it is indispensable for your opposite numbers to feel that you are genuinely interested in them as people and in their views. That is how serious nations engage in professional statecraft. And that is how most significant gifts come to fruition.

OVERCOMING ECONOMIC BAD NEWS AND PSYCHOLOGICAL RESISTANCE

It is important to keep in mind that major donations derive from accumulated "surplus capital." Generally such donations are not imperiled by shallow recessions, minor downward swings in the stock market, instability abroad, the relative value of real estate, or the price of oil.

Wealthy people enjoy diversified portfolios. Their investment strategies hedge against such downside risks.

To be sure, the economic outlook may affect the psychology of the donor or the prospect. And a dip in the gross domestic product or the Dow might be used as a pretext for saying no to an ask or even to a meeting.

Don't let such passing conditions become a reason to slow the pace of your solicitations, and don't take no for an answer, at least not a permanent one. Persistence pays off.

The practice of fundraising is not unlike other professional endeavors. In writing about the ingredients of success in politics, Chris Matthews uses language that any development director, volunteer solicitor, or chief executive must understand and internalize:

> You need to be able to face rejection, hostility, and, more often, indifference. The higher your ambitions take you, the more stamina you'll need, the more willing to get a "NO!" slammed in your face. The more failure you can accept, the greater your chance of success. Whatever your ambition, you can't win unless you are in the game. To win the contest, you first have to be a contestant.[16]

TO ASK: POPPING THE QUESTION

Truly, there is never a bad season of the year, time of day, or economic climate in which to raise funds for a worthy cause or institution.

Ask. Ask early. Ask often. And learn from your hits and your misses.

In my opinion, there is much more talk about asking for money—its challenges, problems, obstacles—than there is in putting the question frankly to the right prospect.

- Would you be willing to help establish a patron's circle with a donation of $5,000?

- Can you see your way to a gift of $100,000 paid out over two or three years?

- Will you join your friend and colleague in giving $500,000 to this worthy and noble cause?

- While we will be grateful for any positive decision you reach, in view of your reputation in the community as a generous benefactor, a lead gift in the $3 to $5 million range would represent a very special vote of confidence in our campaign. Will you consider such a gift?

Practice popping the question. Only by doing so face to face and with regularity will the act of asking become comfortable. Think of it this way: Those wealthy prospects across the desk will be disappointed if you don't request a gift worthy of their means. Don't let them down!

First-rate fundraisers truly believe that requesting a charitable gift is a favor to potential donors. It offers the prospect the chance to move from worldly success to social consequence. It provides a medium to move beyond self-interest to helping others. There is growing evidence that people who give generously of their time and treasure are healthier, physically and psychologically, and live longer than those who do not.[17]

If giving is so good in so many ways for the donor, then asking is both a favor and an act of flattery. Why would you wish to deprive anyone of the benefits that accrue from helping others?

Many people tremble at the mere thought of asking for a charitable donation. They fear rejection. They worry about compromising their friendships or their relationship with clients. The very process seems awkward and uncomfortable. Besides, if you overcome successfully all of these hesitancies and are successful, your reward, more often than not, is to be asked for a donation yourself. Yesterday's target of opportunity becomes today's solicitor of you. And that common expectation of reciprocity can be both habit forming and expensive.

You need, then, to really believe in the cause or organization on behalf of which you seek funds, enough to be very generous in relation to your means. When asking someone you know for a gift to charity, no argument is more convincing than citing your own donation and no words are more compelling than "please join me."

To overcome any inhibition, remember you are not asking for yourself but for others. Imagine the difference it will make—the suffering that will be eased, the children who will be taught, the shelter that will be provided, or the art that will be created if your prospect says yes.

And always remember what this eleemosynary act will do for the donor. How it will provide a meaning beyond self, a sense of satisfaction mere material goods cannot supply, a connection to a wider world. Just as Peace Corps volunteers frequently attest that they received more than they gave on their tour of duty, so donors find that giving does not hurt. Far from it. Charitable contributions soothe the soul, gratify the ego, satisfy curiosities, and impress neighbors and colleagues far more than the private plane, the larger yacht, the third home, or the extravagant, over-the-top party or vacation.

What is more, giving is at least as much an exercise of the heart as it is of the mind. How else to explain why Harvard, Yale, and Princeton alums continue to donate generously when endowments to their alma maters totaled, by year-end 2007, $34.6 billion, $22.5 billion, and $15.8 billion, respectively? That's about $2 million, $1.8 million, and $2.2 million, respectively, per student.[18] Indeed, Yale and Princeton now draw annual income from their respective endowments that amount to roughly 45 percent of their total annual operating budgets. Harvard, a much larger institution, is not far behind in approaching that extraordinary proportion.

Making the intellectual case that these institutions need more philanthropic funds is becoming tougher and tougher. It may also be beside the point. Students and alumni form a psychological bond with their school. Properly understood, emotion rules. That is why alums who belonged to fraternities, sports teams, or performing arts groups, or were recruited to the firms that employ them through a university network, tend to give far more than those whose only memory of their university experience is contained in the framed degree on their study wall at home.

If you can create a context in which donors can enjoy memorable experiences, encounters, connections, and relationships, you, too, will have struck a responsive, emotional chord in them. Doing so is an attribute given only to extraordinary places and to gifted fundraisers.

QUALITIES OF EXCELLENT FUNDRAISERS

First-class solicitors are energetic, self-confident, and curious people. They enjoy meeting others and learning about them. They relish solving the puzzle of how best to match a prospect's interests and resources with a nonprofit's mission and needs.

First-class fundraisers enjoy learning. They listen carefully. They possess a zest for social engagement. Resilient in the face of disappointment and setbacks, prizewinning solicitors project optimism and enjoy a sense of humor.

They are poised, not easily rattled or intimidated. They are resourceful and determined. They communicate very well, orally and in writing.

The best fundraisers inspire confidence and loyalty. They know how to work with others on their team—the trustees, the board and campaign chair, development colleagues and other influentials.

They are creative (head in the sky) and practical (feet planted firmly on the ground).

It is a mystery to me, then, as to why relatively few presidents of important nonprofits emerge from the ranks of superb development directors. To be sure, hospitals may require an MD of its CEO and universities a PhD of theirs. Still, I am struck by how relatively rare it has been for search firms and search committees to look to development professionals as part of the pool of CEO candidates. No one who knows the following leaders, all of whom have emerged from the ranks of fundraisers, can doubt that the Russell Reynolds, Spencer Stuarts, and Heidrick & Struggles of this world should pay heed!

- Claudia Bonn, formerly executive director, Film Society of Lincoln Center and currently executive director, Wave Hill Conservancy

- Kathy Brown, formerly executive director, Jazz at Lincoln Center and currently chief operating officer, WNYC Radio

- Jane Gullong, executive director, New York City Opera

- Karen Hopkins, president, Brooklyn Academy of Music

- Gregory Long, president, New York Botanical Garden

- Emily K. Rafferty, president, Metropolitan Museum of Art

- Arlene Schuler, president, City Center

READY, SET, ASK

The wealth is all around you. Social needs are compelling. There are limits to what government, acting alone, can finance or accomplish. Having worked hard to recruit and motivate a devoted cadre of generous volunteers and a devoted board of directors and having hired a staff possessed of the proper skills, temperament, and attitude, you are really ready for the most significant and difficult part of fundraising: the face-to-face solicitation.

CHAPTER 3

ASKING, FACE TO FACE

Listening, not imitation, maybe the sincerest form of flattery. . . .
If you want to influence someone, listen to what he says.

—Dr. Joyce Brothers

The weakest ink is more powerful than the strongest memory.

—Anonymous

The toughest challenge in fundraising is securing an appointment for a face-to-face solicitation. Succeed in doing so and the likelihood of getting to yes improves dramatically. Most people find it difficult to say no in your presence. It is much harder to turn down a request when you are in the room with the fundraiser than to do so by mail or telephone. Do all you can to schedule a meeting.

In seeking major gifts, remember that there is no substitute for the peer-to-peer, face-to-face solicitation. Naomi Levine, a legendary fundraiser for New York University, puts it this way: "You don't raise major gifts by postage stamps. You do it by shoe leather."

Meetings enable you to determine what your prospect is really about. Through verbal and nonverbal communication, you can tell whether your ideas are taking hold, capturing attention, grabbing an imagination, or whether it is time to change course and try another direction. You can sense whether your prospect is willing and able to reach a decision now, or soon, or whether substantially more time is required. And you can determine whether you have the right companion(s) on your solicitation team or if a substitution or two is in order.

When you need to raise a great deal of money to balance your operating budget or to satisfy a capital campaign, the major challenge is scheduling enough appointments every week. By comparison, preparing your oral presentation and written follow-up, conducting detailed donor research, and rehearsing "the ask" with your team is relatively easy.

If the prospect knows and has enjoyed meaningful engagement with your organization, the likelihood of landing an appointment increases appreciably.

The odds are even better if the request for a meeting comes from a close friend, a social companion, or a business associate.

Even under such conditions, one often hears reasons like these not to ask for an appointment or not to receive a positive reply to a request:

- I'm beset with too many requests right now. I'm overcommitted.

- Your cause just isn't a priority for me. I'm donating my finite resources to other charitable endeavors.

- Now is a bad time to see me.

- Asking to see me is a mistake. You have bigger fish to fry.

- I don't just wish to contribute financially. I'd like to be involved.

- Why do charities keep appealing, over and over again, to the same potential donors? Surely there are others out there who can help.

All of those explanations for not being involved financially can be dealt with comfortably at a well-planned meeting when you are accompanied by a committed donor well known to your prospect.

Some explanations do not involve whether to give or be solicited but when, how much, and spread out over what period of time.

Some of them assume that you are looking for the largest donor or a lead benefactor rather than a major contributor.

Others assume that all you want is cash or securities and will not be prepared to discuss involvement in the life of the institution, varying all the way from assuming a meaningful volunteer role to becoming a member of the board of directors.

The ostensible sources of resistance, rationales, excuses, are pretty standard. Don't let them discourage you from landing that absolutely critical face-to-face encounter.

Nowadays, those who are asked to such meetings often feign a lack of desire. More often than not, they are flattered that you and one or more very important figures in their lives are reserving time to see them. More often than not, they are very curious about what you have to say. And almost always they know precisely why you wish to meet.

Mrs. Vincent Astor was fond of telling solicitors that she knew exactly why they had asked to see her. In encouraging them not to be shy and to "get on with it," she quoted these lines:

> There was a young lady of Kent
> Who said that she knew what it meant
> When men asked her to dine,
> And served cocktails and wine
> She knew what it meant—but she went!

Keep today's ladies and gentlemen of Kent and elsewhere as busy as possible.

APPOINTMENT SECURED: NOW WHAT?

In my experience, at least on a first call, one need not forecast that funds will be solicited. Indeed, they may well not be. Rather, I often ask prospects whether they would be willing to learn about recent major developments at Lincoln Center or offer guidance on several of the important challenges on our horizon.

I never ask an administrative assistant to arrange a meeting unless the prospect has expressed a willingness to me or another team member directly. I always place my own phone calls. I never leave a prospect on hold waiting for me to pick up the phone. I express my preference to meet wherever and whenever pleases the prospect and although I never request more than an hour, our team is delighted if more time is desired. Never, ever arrive late for an agreed-upon appointment.

When meeting a prospect, it is preferable to begin by asking questions about how he or she or the family or business is faring or about a common interest (a politician, a country club, a civic issue, a shared board involvement). People enjoy talking about themselves if the expression of interest is genuine. Such informal conversation relaxes everyone and allows you to ease into the subject at hand in a natural, unforced manner.

If it appears that your prospect is ready for an ask, proceed in this way: Be specific. Be clear. Be deliberate. State your actual expectation unhesitatingly. And, then wait for an answer. Too many solicitors feel nervous and awkward and step into the silence with an apology, a caveat, an inadvertent excuse for the potential donor to delay. Keeping eye contact after the detailed request and keeping quiet requires discipline. It is not easy. But it works.

PLEASE AND THANK YOU

The magic words in fundraising are *please* and *thank you*.

Please, uttered by the right contact, got you through the door.

You have arranged for that already committed customer, client, social, or professional peer to ask for a specific sum from a well-qualified prospect.

On very rare occasions, you will hit pay dirt immediately. More often the response will be "Let me think about it," or "I'm of a mind to do something here, but I'm not quite sure what," or "I'll discuss your request with my spouse."

The follow-up to any meeting must be fast. Debrief with your team immediately, if possible in the lobby of the office building where you met the prospect.

In any of the cases just cited, its time to invoke the thank you, orally and then in writing, preferably on the very day of your fundraising visit.

Be sure your donor or active prospect knows how much you appreciate his or her time and attention.

DONOR RECOGNITION: HERE TO STAY

There are a limited number of ways to express appreciation to individuals, foundations, and corporations for the generosity they offer. Often their gifts make possible the quality we value at the university, on the operating table, in the research laboratory, or at the museum. Money, alas, is the mother's milk responsible for much that we value in an advocate's voice, a think tank's study, or a social service well delivered.

So I find it especially churlish of those who enjoy the benefits of such gifts to complain that they are associated with naming opportunities of programs, professorships, or buildings, rather than being blessed only by donors who prefer anonymity.

Of course, one is entitled to expect the tasteful application of a donor's name to an activity or a facility. No doubt excess can be found.

Charles Isherwood, writing in Sunday's *New York Times* of December 2, 2007, is one of the latest to complain. He calls donor recognition "the graffiti of the philanthropic class" and wonders whatever happened to Anonymous.

I notice that above the title of this article is Mr. Isherwood's byline. Hmm. Whatever happened to anonymity?

Surely what is good for the benefactor's goose is good for the journalist's gander.

Is it awful for a donor to want grandchildren to know of the philanthropy he or she dispensed?

How can a corporation offering a substantial gift to a charity explain a "passion for anonymity" to a shareowner expecting some benefit to the firm from a nonprofit transaction?

Donor recognition is rooted in natural human and institutional impulses. So is a journalist's quest for identity and recognition, if not fame.

They are here to stay. Three cheers.

MERIT MATTERS: THE FORMAL WRITTEN REQUEST

Now you need to establish a compelling case in writing that is concise, simply stated, and persuasive.

Donors relish choice. They do not like to be presented with a single idea. If you put them in a position of "fund it or leave it," they are far more likely to say no.

Too many nonprofits inadvertently fall into the trap of the one-and-only ask. For example, if we have a new program at Lincoln Center that requires support, our development staff sets a restricted grant target for its funding. But unrestricted gifts are fungible. We are free to move them from place to place as the institution's needs require.

Never impose your current priority on a prospect. Offer it, but be prepared to provide many alternatives. Getting to yes means presenting multiple ways to elicit an affirmative response.

Illustratively, I have noticed that people of a certain age generally fall into two categories.

There are those over 60 whom, having enjoyed for themselves the benefits of high-quality institutions like the 92nd Street Y, the International Rescue Committee, or Lincoln Center, now desire to strengthen their favorite for the next generation of beneficiaries.

In the forefront of their minds are two questions:

1. What can I do to leave an organization or cause I care about better able to serve the needs of my children and grandchildren and their peers?

2. How can I deploy my donations in a way that will leave an enduring legacy?

But there are those in the same age cohort possessed of a very different point of view. They are focused on seeing the seeds of their giving blossom while they are likely to be alive to enjoy them. These folks are, by their own admission, interested in short-term gratification.

They do not buy green bananas. Sometimes childless, they are not preoccupied with the long term. They live in the present, or, having left their children in excellent financial shape, they do not believe it is their obligation or even prerogative to set philanthropic priorities for them. Their kids are perfectly capable of selecting for themselves the institutions or causes that are worthy of philanthropic investment.

When preparing a written proposal to an individual or institutional prospect that offers no guidelines or restrictions as to form, keep it short, keep it simple, and keep it exciting. And offer choices. Donor motivations and intent are complex and variable. Providing alternatives invites the participation of your prospect in a decision. Besides, it is more difficult to decide negatively on two or more alternatives than to say no to what may be perceived as a take-it-or-leave-it approach.

Donors are also busy people. Any idea or program can be stated briefly and can bring the reader to the point quickly. If the prospect wants more detail, rest assured, you will be asked for it. More often than not, nonprofits err on the side of excess, intimidating donors with too much written material and losing the opportunity to convey the essence of the request.

The central question any proposal needs to answer is: Why are my (institution's) funds needed? Or: What difference will my support really make? Prospects need to be persuaded that in the absence of their favorable response, something important will not happen at all, or not happen on time, or happen with less quality than it would have otherwise.

Unless a solicitation generates interest by offering a compelling reason to give, one that appeals to the heart of the donor and not just the mind, it will fall short of hitting a bull's-eye. Behind many declinations is the prospect's sense that what is being requested can be acquired elsewhere or is prosaic, a milquetoast kind of request. Only indiscreet donors will tell you so, but that is often how they feel.

THE LURE OF THE CHALLENGE GRANT

One sure-fire technique for proving how much a donor's gift matters is the challenge grant connected to a firm deadline. For example, in direct mail, a named presolicited donor offers a gift of up to a specified (preferably six- or seven-figure) sum, but only if others donate the equivalent by a certain date. The same method can be used in face-to-face approaches to individuals, foundations, and corporations. The suggestion that a donor is willing to match a prospect's gift often stimulates a positive response. Everyone enjoys knowing that their gift is being magnified by the generosity of another donor. The challenge grant conveys a message that the benefactor is more than simply generous: He or she is offering indispensable leadership.

If it can be said that fundraising resembles a science, that science is psychology. One of the major challenges confronting any fundraising team is maintaining momentum and motivation through the completion of a project or a campaign.

Often finding a donor prepared to challenge others to match his or her contribution is a terrific way to ignite a fundraising drive. There are many variations on the theme. A donor can tender a gift only on the condition that it be matched three or four or five to one by trustees, or by corporations, or by foundations, or by direct mail donors, or by proceeds of a special event, or by any combination of these.

As such, the challenge grant remains an extraordinarily successful and pliable form of leverage. Deployed in timely fashion, it can help take a campaign either out of the doldrums or over the top.

THE GENERATIONAL DIVIDE

Those who give large sums to nonprofits are disproportionately old(er) while the professionals paid to raise those sums are very much younger. The age disparity is often as much as 20 to 40 years. That gap can engender occasional tension, dismay, and humor.

Younger professionals tend to be familiar, calling people they hardly know by their first names in writing or in person. For mature adults, the right to call someone by a first name is earned over time.

Such informality also characterizes the way young professionals communicate. They tend to (over)use email, whereas their donors would often welcome an old-fashioned letter. By the way, the letter ought to be well written, shorn of misspellings and typographical errors, and it should come to the point in crisp prose.

Donors expect to be treated not as customers or suppliers handling a commercial transaction, but as citizens engaged in private action for the public good. They are annoyed and offended when a charitable pledge they have advanced to a nonprofit organization is followed up not by a letter of warm appreciation requesting its redemption but by a brusque note enclosing an "invoice."

An invoice? That's an itemized bill, a detailed list of goods or services rendered, with an account of all costs.

What is the relevance of such language to an act of philanthropy?

Donors, generally, rise very early in the morning. Many have read the newspapers—the *New York Times*, the *Wall Street Journal*, the *Financial Times*—before their breakfast meetings scheduled for 7:30 or 8:00. Fundraising staff who are single seem generally unaccustomed to being roused out of bed at such an uncivilized time of day. Parents with children have their hands full with domestic chores before they can leave home for work. In both cases, being able to converse with a donor about a news story or editorial in that morning's newspaper is out of the question.

There are at least two points worth noting about these lifestyle contrasts.

1. The disparity between generations is not new. 'Twas ever thus, although in the high-tech twenty-first century it assumes new, intriguing forms.

2. It is always the solicitors who need to cross the generational divide to encounter their donors. Always. The donors are right, by definition. They deserve to receive information in a form congenial to them. They should be thanked graciously for their generosity, not billed or dunned for an offered gift. Meeting them halfway is 50 percent less than what is required to be successful.

In short, nonprofits must tailor the timing and the form of their conduct to the preferences of donors and prospects. There is simply no room for self-indulgent behavior on the part of the solicitor.

CONFESSIONS OF A CEO

Fundraising is just one of many organizational activities requiring a chief executive's leadership and management.

One of a CEO's recurring challenges is deciding when and how deeply to intervene in a process or an interaction.

In the classic model, CEOs recruit and assess their direct reports, reward and recognize them, formulate strategy, set stretch goals to be met, and then hold senior executives accountable.

I know and even admire presidents and executive directors who conduct themselves exactly in this manner. They do not allow themselves to be mired in detail. They separate themselves from the day-to-day life of the organization. Set strategy. Focus on governance. Keep the big picture in mind. These are the bywords of the hands-off chief executive.

I have never been employed by an organization that did not seem to need more, much more, of its CEO. Nonprofits, generally even those of formidable size, are not so richly staffed as to allow their executive leaders to stay away from operational matters.

Besides, very often the prospective donor, the inquisitive reporter, the key government official or politician, the indispensable partner, or the important trustee expects to receive attention not from the development director, public relations director, public affairs manager, or head of business initiatives but from the CEO and only the CEO.

On one end of the spectrum is the relatively remote, orderly, inaccessible, and somewhat intimidating CEO for whom delegation is less a management method than a way of life. Rarely can such a figure add much value to fundraising. By its very nature, raising funds is a highly personal, labor-intensive enterprise, demanding time and attention and filled with surprising twists and turns.

On the other end of the spectrum is the hands-on CEO, one who borders on micromanaging and who fails to trust staff to step up to a demanding standard of high performance.

Finding the right balance between these two prototypes is a CEO's lot.

The hands-off CEO wonders why the boss should be the only one permitted to make mistakes, to fail on occasion. Depriving staff of such opportunities may avoid an error, but it also removes a chance to learn and grow professionally.

For the hands-on CEO, there is a difference between delegation and abdication, and there are many occasions when CEO engagement is a critical success factor in achieving a positive outcome.

Identifying which situations really require personal intervention and which can be left for others to work out on their own is a matter of judgment and often a tough call.

I know I personally err on the side of doing too much.

Suffice it to say, I am still learning.

I have overheard it said on more than one occasion that "the terrific thing about Reynold is that he knows a lot about fundraising and he is willing and able to help set and reach ambitious objectives." But I have also heard it said that "the tough thing about Reynold is exactly that he knows a lot about fundraising." From the point of vantage of the vice president for development and her staff, reporting to a president fluent in the fundraising process and willing to be an integral part of it is a mixed blessing.

Notwithstanding the occasional downside of presidential involvement, generally I have found that my errors have been more of omission than commission. When matters have gone awry, more often than not, I have repressed my instinct to act at all or did not act soon enough. Such situations include:

- Allowing a staff member to engage with a trustee for too long a time when it should have been clear that the relationship was not working and could not be repaired.

- Hiring an employee not up to the job and failing to acknowledge the error and find a replacement promptly.

- Permitting a campaign director to accompany a trustee on a funding call not to the corporate CEO and not even to a senior officer but to a low-on-the-totem-poll staffer formally in charge of philanthropy. That's a recipe for entanglement in business bureaucracy and should be avoided, if at all possible. Do everything you can to see the CEO or his or her closest colleagues about your request. Otherwise, the likelihood of success is vastly reduced. I saw it coming. I let it happen. Mea culpa.

It pains me to recall these mistakes. It helps to know that every new day since, I have had the chance to avoid repeating them. After all, there are new versions of them just around the corner, no doubt.

One definite error to avoid is failing to place a high priority on hiring staff skilled in written communication. Fine writing is a prizewinning virtue at Lincoln Center.

THE WRITTEN PROPOSAL: A PRIZEWINNING EXAMPLE

Alas, rarely at Lincoln Center, or elsewhere, are the highest standards of excellence met in the grant proposals churned out daily. Let me show you one that in my judgment passes this test with flying colors.

The case we needed to build was not easy. Lincoln Center required funds for its Lincoln Center Festival 2008, in general, and for the production of a very expensive, hardly ever performed opera, in particular. The festival as a whole and the opera, in particular, *Die Soldaten*, present daunting obstacles to funding.

These events are extremely expensive. Typically, ticket sales offset no more than 25 to 35 percent of the costs, leaving the balance to be raised. What is more, the festival offers esoteric music, dance, theater, site-specific installations, and multimedia productions. They emanate from countries most people have not visited or cannot even locate on a map. They are frequently drawn from centuries past. They are presented in the original language, not English. The audiences learn what is going on by viewing subtitles or hearing translations via earphones.

Productions are mounted in the most authentic manner. Meeting that objective often involves huge costs: supporting ensembles such as an orchestra, chorus, or dance company; extravagant staging; and extensive rehearsal time. Frequently, the events presented are long, with running times between two and a half to ten hours. And, to make the situation even more challenging, the subject matter is truly foreign, far from the experience of the New Yorker, the American tourist, or the overseas visitor.

It is no wonder that many we approach consider the festival an expensive extravaganza. Particularly in a country increasingly characterized by limited attention spans, linguistic and cultural illiteracy, and a desire to flee to the familiar, one can hardly be unsympathetic to such a point of view.

In the face of all these obstacles to eliciting help, the content and style of the proposal and to whom it is sent matters a great deal. As you read the actual document we sent out, ask yourself these questions:

- Does the proposal adequately explain the context for the presentation of *Die Soldaten* by describing the Lincoln Center Festival compellingly?

- Does the proposal explain persuasively why Lincoln Center would wish to present this extensive and expensive piece that is both artistically challenging and logistically daunting?

- Are you impressed by the citation of specific details to characterize the work of art and its progeny?

- Are you moved by the idea of bringing this production to New York City and having audiences experience it in a magnificent new space never before used for mounting opera?

Take a look. As you do, please note that there is virtually no difference between how the proposal would be crafted whether it is destined for the eyes of a foundation official, a corporate executive, or an individual donor. Indeed, the same disciplined explanation of the case for funding would work for requesting smaller gifts as well regardless of the field of endeavor. Solid, engaged, and persuasive writing knows no bounds. It is rarely exhibited. It is welcomed by all recipients.

DIE SOLDATEN

LINCOLN CENTER FESTIVAL 2008

Since its inaugural season in 1996, the Lincoln Center Festival has become respected worldwide as the broadest and most original performing arts program in Lincoln Center's history. In 12 seasons, the series has presented over 1,000 performances by artists from more than 50 countries, commissioning nearly 30 new works and offering more than 110 world, U.S., and New York premieres.

The Lincoln Center Festival also expands the scope of the campus' programming by showcasing contemporary artistic viewpoints and multidisciplinary works that defy categorization. Drawing upon Lincoln Center's unique strengths and resources, the Festival is able to present major companies and large-scale productions that might not otherwise appear in New York City. The Festival has regularly stretched the possibilities of Lincoln Center's theaters, whether by pouring 40,000 gallons of water on the stage of the New York State Theater in *Writing to Vermeer*, or creating a Japanese stage complete with a depiction of the Pacific Ocean in Avery Fisher Hall for *Pacific Overtures*, or by building completely new theaters in Damrosch Park for Ariane Mnouchkine's Theatre de Soleil or Nakamura Kanzaburo's Heisei Nakamura-za.

Beginning July 5, 2008, the Lincoln Center Festival will launch its thirteenth season with five performances of Bernd Alois Zimmermann's landmark opera *Die Soldaten*. New York audiences will experience the work through the production directed by David Pountney, first performed at Germany's Ruhr Triennale Music Festival in 2006. The opera will be mounted in

Manhattan's Seventh Regiment Armory in what will be the most dramatic production, and the first opera, ever to be performed in this space.

Die Soldaten is one of the rare iconic operas of the second half of the twentieth century, more talked about in opera circles than seen, whose challenges are of such proportions that each production is spoken of in very special terms as, for example, "the Boston production" or the "Rhoda Levine production." Famously, the first version of this opera was rejected by its commissioner, the Cologne Opera House, as unrealizable. Though Zimmerman later revised the score, he still defied the conventions of opera by calling for far more percussion than could fit in any standard orchestra pit and for an array of 15 scenes that meld into one another in a cinematic way that has always stretched the resources of every director who has tackled this grand opera. Nonetheless, *Die Soldaten* has earned a reputation as the major German opera of the second half of the twentieth century and one whose message expresses, perhaps more than any other work of music theater, the pain and anguish of the Second World War.

Zimmermann drew his inspiration for the work from the 1775 play of the same name by the German poet Jakob Lenz. The opera, set in Lille and Armentires in French Flanders, tells the story of Marie, a young woman whose reputation, and, subsequently, her life, are ruined by the philandering of officers and, finally, the depravity of common soldiers. In the final scene, the action builds to the cataclysm that results when any one human is abandoned to the ruthless power of a group of soldiers for whom morality holds no sway.

The music itself has much to do with the work's devoted following in the opera world. Zimmerman uses a variety of styles and techniques to create a work of visceral impact. An admirer of Alban Berg, Zimmermann employs what was at the time the most advanced compositional idiom of serialism and twelve-tone technique, while simultaneously referencing antecedents from Bach cantatas to jazz. The composer also calls for extraordinary vocal performances from his singers as well as for pre-recorded sounds, amplified voices, and film.

Yet the most groundbreaking aspect of *Die Soldaten* is most certainly its staging, which is unlike that of any other opera of its kind. In addition to the sixteen singing and ten speaking roles, the opera requires a one-hundred-piece orchestra involving many unusual instruments and pieces of percussion. Every production of *Die Soldaten* has had to wrestle with the challenges inherent in the work. How can the orchestra be divided to accommodate the percussion requirements? How can the scenes be made coherent when one flows so immediately into another? The orchestra issue has always been solved by placing percussionists in another room and bringing their sounds to the auditorium electronically. Various uses of film and split stages have been used to accommodate the staging concerns.

The production directed by David Pountney solves the problems in a very different way that has been hailed by the press as "a restoration of triumphal status" (*Die Zeit*), doing "justice to *Die Soldaten* for perhaps the first time in 40 years" (*Die Welt*). Pountney, who rose to fame as one of the triumvirate leaders of the English National Opera (ENO), where he served as production director from 1982 to 1993, is credited for mounting legendary productions that squarely reestablished the ENO as one of the creative centers for opera in England. He now directs opera for many companies in Europe and is the Intendant of the Bregenz Festival in Austria.

Lincoln Center's production as directed by Pountney centers on a moving stage, constructed to accommodate Zimmerman's theatrical vision of an opera in which time, place and action are juxtaposed. The entire orchestra surrounds the audience, percussion on one side, the bulk of the orchestra on the other. The audience, straddling both sides of a stage that is essentially a very long, narrow platform, is literally moved on railroad tracks, so that at times the singers are seen from a great distance, and at other times they appear to be very near. The effect is so disorienting that many members of the audience in Bochum had no idea that they themselves were moving, falsely believing instead that it was the stage that was in motion like a conveyor belt, alternately creating panoramic backdrops or drawing them into the action.

Given the production demands of *Die Soldaten*, Lincoln Center will present the work at the Seventh Regiment Armory, on East 68th street and Park Avenue in Manhattan—the first opera ever to be performed in that space. Measuring approximately 200 by 300 feet, with an 80-foot-high barrel vault ceiling, the Armory is one of the few venues in New York that is well able to accommodate the artistic and technical complexities of this opera. Built in 1879 as the regimental organization of the U.S. National Guard, the Armory is now overseen by the Seventh Regiment Armory Conservancy—a not-for-profit coalition of philanthropists and civic leaders whose mission it is to restore the Armory's physical structure while making it accessible to the public through the presentation of visual and performing arts events. For the Armory, the mounting of *Die Soldaten* will be part of its long-term goal of transforming itself into a dynamic cultural and education center; for Lincoln Center, partnering with the Armory represents an ambitious effort to continue to expand the scope and reach of the institution's programming beyond the confines of its 16-acre campus.

David Pountney's production of *Die Soldaten* received unanimous acclaim at the Ruhr Triennale in 2006. The German press called it "a true sensation which will go down in the history of opera." The performance of soprano Claudia Barainsky, who played Marie and is expected to reprise the role for Lincoln Center next summer, was described as "magnificent both vocally as well as dramatically." But perhaps the most important aspect of this production is that its impact on the audience is immediate and profound. The greatest accolade came from the *Financial Times of London*, which called it "a knuckle-whitening ride through a thrilling tale . . . A complex tale so clearly narrated that there is never an instant's confusion as to what is really happening . . . a site-specific performance experience that no conventional house could emulate." As a centerpiece of the 2008 Lincoln Center Festival, *Die Soldaten* is certain to once again offer audiences a gripping and unforgettable theatrical experience.

Clearly, a limited number of sources might be interested in helping Lincoln Center mount *Die Soldaten*. But with the application of some energy and imagination, more than you would imagine readily come to mind.

First, of course, are the opera aficionados who already know of the piece and would enjoy seeing it presented by Lincoln Center. Of that group, only a much smaller subset would even entertain "paying for the privilege" in the form of a handsome donation. Count them on the fingers of two or three hands.

Second, there is the German government, local and national, proud of this mid-twentieth-century work and eager for American audiences to see the David Pountney production, first performed at Germany's Ruhr Triennale Music Festival in 2006.

Third, there are major German corporations, such as Siemens or Volkswagen or Deutsche Bank, which might respond affirmatively to an appeal.

Fourth, there are donors interested not in the specifics of either the Lincoln Center Festival or *Die Soldaten* but by the conversion of Manhattan's Seventh Regiment Armory from a deteriorating, underutilized space for the National Guard to a new visual and performing arts venue in a city that vies to be the cultural capital of the world. If Lincoln Center can successfully mount such an ambitious undertaking as *Die Soldaten* in what is also known as the Park Avenue Armory space, won't others follow, such as the New York City Opera, the Metropolitan Opera, and the like? *Die Soldaten* is a test case for the Armory's viability as a versatile performing arts space. This angle is worth pursuing with lovers of that space or with Eastsiders who would like to animate their rather staid neighborhood.

Finally, the *Die Soldaten* proposal may serve only to open a door to dialogue. Lincoln Center would be perfectly content to receive funding for any other event being presented as part of Festival 2008, or for the festival as a whole, or, more generally, for the institution that year in, year out recognizes the richness of nonwestern cultures and brings them to appreciative audiences and critics. Many donors may quibble with one element of a given festival and find it not to their taste. Fewer take issue with the enterprise as a whole and fail to admire it, grudgingly or otherwise.

Even with the limited appeal of a mid-twentieth-century German opera, we could identify five target groups of prospects. Cover letters custom-designed to appeal to that dimension of *Die Soldaten*'s revival most attractive to a targeted audience were developed. And extensive efforts were also undertaken to identify who knows whom among our prospects so that they could be reached by Lincoln Center loyalists who are also their friends and colleagues.

I have intentionally chosen a very difficult project for which to seek funding in order to illuminate how best to reach donors in writing and to reveal the kind of thought process that leads to excellent proposals accompanied by custom-designed cover letters to specific sources. Proposals so conceived and letters so drafted are a necessary, but not sufficient, condition for success. Sufficiency resides in identifying the right people who know the prospect or whose representations on behalf of Lincoln Center would impress that source. The construction of a meritorious case transmitted by the right "who knows who" usually is unbeatable.

OBSTACLES TO OVERCOME

There will be a tendency for your staff to err on the side of comprehensiveness, detail, and specificity. These proposal attributes are more in the mind of the beholder than of the prospect. They often come at a very significant cost: delay.

In my experience, from a donor's perspective, it is better to be "roughly right," concise, and early than "perfect," long, and late. Those you have solicited are very busy people. If there is a significant gap in time between the stimulus of a meeting and the response of a proposal, other matters will fill the vacuum. Regaining a prospect's attention, once lost, becomes an additional and unnecessary struggle.

Beyond avoiding prolixity and lateness, the proposal's content needs to be crafted from the donor in, not from the supplicant out. In other words, shaping the content of the case to appeal to what interests the specific donor you are soliciting and incorporating what might have been said at your meeting in the written follow-up are critical to success.

Major donors expect and deserve to be treated as unique and to feel that their views, questions, and observations were heard.

Just as research on the donor's background—family, academic, business, net wealth—must be highly particularized, so, too, must all oral and written communication.

INDIVIDUAL DONOR CHECKLIST: SOME VITAL QUESTIONS

No review of the tricks of the fundraising trade is ever complete. Every day, for every nonprofit, there should be new lessons to learn. To help challenge you, to help you prepare, consider the vital questions that conclude this chapter.

1. Are you prepared to offer alternative ways for your prospect to respond favorably in the event he or she is not of a mind to say yes to the first request?

2. Have you considered asking your prospect to help leverage his or her donation and assume philanthropic leadership by offering a challenge to your fundraising team?

3. What criteria have you used to select the one or two volunteers who accompany you on a funding call?

4. You have held your face-to face-solicitation. You have followed up with a warm thank-you letter and a cogent, persuasive written proposal. Now what?

5. How do you accelerate donor progression up the ladder of generosity? What is your plan for donor retention and enhancement?

6. Do you treat your cadre of supporters as allies in your cause?

7. What methods do you employ to engage trustees in the fundraising process?

8. How do you and your colleagues learn to improve your fundraising skills and your track record of success, over time?

9. Are you spending adequate time with existing donors and potential prospects between asks?

10. In what ways does your approach to corporations and foundations differ from how you handle individual prospects at meetings or in written follow-up?

The tenth question on this list sets the scene for what Chapter 4 is all about.

CHAPTER 4

THE INSTITUTIONAL DONOR: CORPORATIONS AND FOUNDATIONS

We invest in our communities for a very simple reason. We live here too.

—Bank of America

If it can be imagined.
It can be done.
This is America.
We never say good enough.
We never say die.

—The CIT Group

Institutional donors are generally more complex creatures than individuals. Their interests are multifaceted, their decision-making processes less transparent and slower, their cast of characters frequently changing, and, in the case of corporations, their stakeholders many and varied.

Figuring them out takes time and endurance. It is not a challenge for a nonprofit's staff only. Your homework should include who knows whom best at these places. It should identify the leading mission and objectives of these institutions and how they intersect with the work of your favorite nonprofit organization or cause.

The effort may be exhausting, but the payoff is handsome. For gifts from companies and foundations carry a seal of approval different from individual donations. Everyone assumes that the competition for institutional support is fierce, that careful due diligence was conducted on the successful organization and its proposal, and that both passed muster in an exacting process.

THE CORPORATION AND THE SMALL BUSINESS

The era of big government is hardly over, but the age of pure corporate philanthropy is drawing to a close. Corporations must justify gifts to charity. Do they enhance the brand, facilitate sound government relations, increase sales, entertain clients, or improve employee morale and loyalty? Find the intersections between nonprofit need and corporate interest and you will unlock the safe not only of what remains as philanthropic funds but of marketing, advertising, sales, sponsorship, and employee relations resources.

In 2007, the Center on Philanthropy of Indiana University estimated corporate contributions to nonprofit institutions to be $15.7 billion. Although that is a large number, it represents only 5 percent of all charitable donations in America. Given its relatively small part of the total, is it prudent for nonprofits to spend an even larger percentage share of their time wooing business support?

The answer is an unequivocal yes.

First of all, corporate support is very different from private foundation and individual giving.

Corporations employ hundreds, even thousands of people in your community. The financial support of a business reinforces or stimulates voluntary activity of all kinds that can satisfy nonprofit needs.

Employees can serve on nonprofit boards of directors or have their own donations matched by the company. They can provide pro bono financial, legal, advertising, public relations, or general management assistance. They can lead fundraising campaigns, chair gala events, or actually be secunded to work for Third Sector organizations on a sabbatical leave or as a bridge to retirement.

A company can authorize the use of facilities, donate surplus or state-of-the-art products or equipment, hire meaningful numbers of graduates of universities or research institutes, and stimulate continuous interaction between beneficiaries and donors.

Because corporations view relationships with nonprofits as adding tangible value to the business, the monetary gains to nonprofits of many of these forms of support are not counted as philanthropy.

Estimates of how much more volunteer support, in-kind gifts, and other kinds of assistance would add to that $15.7 billion figure range widely from 25 percent to 75 percent.

Indeed, in recent years, corporate partnership activity has blossomed so dramatically that a new vocabulary has developed to describe it.

THE PARLANCE OF CORPORATE AID

Cause-related marketing is the label given to instances in which a company "adopts" a charitable institution or movement and builds it into advertising, marketing, and branding efforts. An example is the strong association of American Express with "saving monuments" around the world and its alignment with international travel and therefore use of credit cards and traveler's checks. The identification of a huge multinational company with helping children and families during pre- and postoperative care in or near your town is perfectly captured by the Ronald McDonald Houses that have been built all around the country. They burnish that company's brand. The association of Rolex or Movado with innovative or cutting-edge performing arts perfectly captures the emphasis of these companies on graceful design and flawless functionality. The emphasis of IBM on the use of technology as a learning tool, particularly although not exclusively in elementary and secondary school settings, has acquainted generations of faculty and students with its hardware and software.

Embedded giving is the name attributed to a gift to charity with every product purchase or as some percentage of the cashier's total, for some specific period of time. This kind of support is spreading quickly, particularly around such holidays as Mother's and Father's days, Valentine's Day, the Fourth of July, Veteran's Day, Thanksgiving, or the winter holiday season. Often associated with advertising, window displays, or point-of-purchase information placards, the causes supported range from the prevention and treatment of breast or prostate cancer, to help for American veterans of war, from antihunger and community center activities, to assisting humanitarian causes by combating the effects of natural disaster or refugee crises.

Corporate sponsorships have expanded by orders of magnitude. These are carefully drawn arrangements, often drafted in legal form, in which a nonprofit agrees to provide specific services in exchange for defined cash or in-kind support.

Universities benefit from research contracts with pharmaceutical companies or high-tech firms. Arts organizations receive much-needed cash and in-kind support in exchange for branding certain programs with the name of the business, or displaying product where patrons and passersby are sure to see it, or receiving complimentary tickets and facility space to entertain customers, or offering employees recognition for their excellent performance.

And you have no doubt noticed the spread of corporate naming arrangements. Either in perpetuity or, more likely for a fixed number of years, some firms have chosen to place their names not only at sports stadiums but on performing arts facilities. The Roundabout's American Airlines Theater in Manhattan is the nonprofit analog to the proprietary deals cut to name for-profit performing arts spaces such as The Ford Theater or The Nokia Theater in the same vicinity. The Wang Center for the Performing Arts near Boston and, most recently, the Carnival Center for the Performing Arts in Miami are conspicuous examples of corporate branding. And so, for that matter, is the Morgan Stanley Children's Hospital at New York-Presbyterian.

These efforts to associate companies with important attributes in the public mind such as trust, caring, integrity, high quality by naming buildings, projects, or programs in an enduring way are part of what has come to be known as corporate branding.

CORPORATE SUPPORT MAGNIFIED

Very few, if any, of these relatively new and expanding arrangements between business and nonprofits are captured by charitable contributions data. Therefore, that $15.7 billion number, or 5 percent charitable market share number, is wildly underestimated.

For example, The Arts Consulting Group reports that sponsorship spending by North American companies in 2007 rose by 10.5 percent to $13.37 billion. Of this sum, about 30 to 40 percent is destined for nonprofit organizations and causes rather than sports and commercial entertainment, two of the largest recipients.[1]

In considering overall charitable giving in America, donations to religious organizations reached $102.3 billion, 40 percent of all giving by individuals and households in 2007 ($252 billion) and 33 percent of the total philanthropic pie when one includes foundations and corporations.[2]

The difference is attributable to the fact that little of foundation giving and virtually none of corporate giving is directed to religious institutions or causes. As a result, while corporate charitable gifts were 5 percent of all charitable donations in 2007, they were double that sum, or 10 percent, of all support to secular or nondenominational organizations.

Putting together this reality with the fact that contributions data fail to capture so much of corporate assistance to nonprofits highlights the desirability of developing a robust corporate solicitation program. When the benefits to businesses are more than "incidental," they are legally not considered donations in intent or result. Therefore, they are not officially recorded as charitable gifts. Similarly, data collection schemes are wholly wanting in capturing what sprawling, decentralized, empowered corporate divisions do for and with the Third Sector.

Under such circumstances, the payoff for pursuing business support becomes very attractive.

SMALL BUSINESS, LARGE IMPACT

But there is even more. An accumulating body of evidence suggests that the fastest-growing segment of philanthropy in the for-profit sector is small and midsize businesses. This nascent trend has been hard to detect. Here's why. The principal sources of data on corporate giving—the Council on Financial Aid to Education, the Conference Board, and the Council on Foundations—have focused almost exclusively on firms with at least 500 employees and $100 million of revenue. Much less is known about the charitable habits of smaller firms than about the Fortune 500, even though such small businesses account for 53 percent of all paid employment in America.

In fact, a fair number of such businesses may take their charitable tax deductions as individuals and not as firms at all, depending on whether they are legally organized as businesses or as partnerships. Many treat their donations as operating expenses or as a part of the cost of goods sold and do not bother taking a charitable tax deduction at all, in any form.

> The strongest factors affecting giving by small companies were the personal values of the owner, the condition of the business, social responsibility, public relations and the quality of the organization making the request.[3]

The more one understands about the owners and managers of these small firms the better, for increasingly they are becoming the new leading actors in business philanthropy. While only 20 percent of Americans are self-employed, 80 percent of America's millionaires describe themselves this way. They are predominantly professionals: lawyers, physicians, consultants, accountants, or small business owners.

It is from the decisions of the burgeoning professional and small business millionaire class and those on their way to joining their rank that charitable contributions increasingly flow. It is in them that great expectations for future growth are placed, for their amassed wealth is simply staggering and unprecedented. Such affluence (in 2006, 9 million people in America enjoy net assets of $1 million or more, exclusive of their homes) renders philanthropic generosity more affordable than ever before in American history. That this already large cohort of millionaire professionals, entrepreneurs, and small business owners is likely to expand from five to seven times faster than the general population is a fundraiser's fantasy come true.[4]

Just one example of the robustness of small business support of nonprofits comes from a Business Committee for the Arts report a decade ago. It found that nearly three-quarters of the total dollars contributed to the arts in 1994 came from companies with $1 million to $50 million in annual revenues.

What a stunning finding, one that is tremendously encouraging to small and emerging arts organizations with limited reach to the huge Fortune 500 firms.

THE CORPORATION: PATHWAY TO AFFLUENT DONORS

Beyond small businesses as an incubator for philanthropy, you should think about the modern corporation as the gateway through which tens of thousands of Americans have been catapulted to affluence by employment at such firms as Intel, Microsoft, Google, Oracle, Sun Microsystems, Yahoo, Netscape, and Goldman Sachs. The wealth of many others has burgeoned due to employment in private equity firms and hedge funds.

Indeed, it can be argued that even the large corporation as benefactor may become less important to nonprofits than the business firm as an identifiable network through which wealth and, it is hoped, charitably generous people can be reached. The nonprofit that sees a business as a medium through which to access a significant and growing number of the affluent as well as a purely institutional source of support will gain a substantial fundraising advantage.

> To put it plainly, the charitable contributions and corporate sponsorship record of Microsoft, Berkshire-Hathaway, Time Warner and Nike, for example, may well matter less to Third Sector organizations than the generosity of their respective chairmen and senior officers—Bill Gates, Warren Buffett, Ted Turner and Phil Knight. They number among the roughly seventy-five members of a relatively new and fast growing "club" in America, one composed exclusively of billionaires. That growing cadre and the some 250,000 American decamillionaires collectively wield far more philanthropic clout than the companies that spawned their wealth.[5]

These words were written in 1999. As I now write eight years later, only the numbers have changed. Today there are 463 billionaires in that club and more than 500,000 decamillionaires. Point made.

To be sure, there is great civic pride around the country, and corporations do express their support for consensus-blessed causes with charitable contributions. In Minneapolis-Saint Paul, the founders of the 5% and 2% Club, where companies pledge that proportion of their pretax net profit to Third Sector organizations and causes, still is a leader in the eleemosynary efforts of business concerns.

In some measure, all companies like reflecting the convictions of their employees. Those employees may leave their valuables behind when they depart from home each morning, but they take their values to the office. And if a company's contribution record helps to attract or retain talent in the bitter-cold winters of Minneapolis-Saint Paul or in any other areas of the country competing for the best and the brightest, that is an inexpensive price for companies to pay.

WINNING BUSINESS SUPPORT

Corporations are not in business to give money away but to earn it for their shareowners. Therefore, "pure" philanthropy given without an agenda or motives of self-interest is relatively rare and unusual. Ask yourself this question: How will corporate philanthropy, or sponsorship or an in-kind gift (advertising, use of facility space, the provision of pro bono services) help to burnish a company's brand, improve employee morale, assist in employee recruitment and retention, advance marketing and sales objectives, or contribute to effective government and community relations?

The most successful recipients of corporate largesse develop allies within firms who advocate on their behalf because they believe both in the nonprofit's mission and in what the business relationship achieves for employees, customers, and owners of common stock. In most transactions with nonprofit institutions, it is expected that corporate interests of one kind or another will be served.

One of the most impressive solicitations I ever experienced as the president of the AT&T Foundation came from the Columbia University School of Engineering. Its delegation included several graduates of the school who were now high-ranking employees of my company's research arm, Bell Laboratories. They could recite the total number of university graduates employed at AT&T and the number (and amount) whose gifts to Columbia were matched by our company. As a prelude to a specific ask, it was clear that the school had done its homework and generated enthusiasm among its graduates for their substantial request of me.

Just as the business firm is different from the individual or the foundation because it can offer a nonprofit a lot more than cash, so, too, the corporation employs multiple decision makers. A development officer can walk through many doors of a corporation and be successful. There are lines of business that are profit and loss centers. But there are also departments of public and government relations, advertising, marketing, and sales that have resources at their disposal which can find their way to you.

As with other prospects, the first challenge is securing favorable, if not privileged, access. Ideally, a member of your board of directors is a senior officer of the company. Alternatively, someone on your board, or among your donors, friends, or colleagues, is a leading customer of the firm. In general, there is nothing to which a company is more responsive than a customer calling on behalf of its favored institution or cause. Time attempting to find clients of the prospect firm whom you may know and who are willing to do your bidding is time very well spent.

Still, although there are many points of entry, there is only one front door, and it leads to the chief executive's suite. No matter what they tell you, no matter how many obstacles they put in the way, endeavor to secure an audience with the corporate chief executive or the highest-ranking officials who report to the CEO. There have been many changes in business in recent decades. At least one rule remains, however: Where you sit in the organizational hierarchy matters, not least when it comes to the disbursement of discretionary resources, such as sponsorships and philanthropy.

But first you need to learn all you can about a company's strategy and its interests. How does each connect to your nonprofit's mission and objectives?

Once you have successfully concluded that homework, you are ready to research who is who inside the firm. Identify the name, rank, and serial number of those responsible for departments that manage assets of potential use to you. Then find out which supporters, friends, and allies of your nonprofit know these folks and can introduce them to your work. Spend time acquainting them with your outfit in person and on-site, in an appealing manner that respects an executive's time and responds to his or her interests.

Such executives and those who know them well might be among your nonprofit's clients or customers. Or they could be neighbors or members of your church or country club. Once you have matched an executive, a small business owner, or a professional who runs his or her own business to someone with whom there is much in common and who admires the work of your nonprofit, you are ready for the ask.

When the time is ripe, recite some of the unmet needs of the organization that can be satisfied with corporate help. Ask whether that is possible. You probably will be astonished by the number and generosity of positive responses to such straightforward, face-to-face requests for help from a nonprofit advocate to a corporate manager or small business owner.

Keeping small businesses in mind is especially important to nonprofits that cannot reach or successfully appeal to large corporations for assistance.

After all, much of small business giving is obligation based. Many small business owners locate their operations in or near their homes. As members in good standing of the community, they generally are responsive to the needs and aspirations of their customers, who are also often friends, suppliers, colleagues, and neighbors.

The appeals of the local Boy and Girl Scout troop, baseball and soccer teams, the community center and the arts ensemble, for example, are difficult to turn away. When loyal customers elicit support for heartfelt causes and concerns, their requests can hardly be ignored or greeted with indifference. Campaigns for United Way, the town social service organization, the Salvation Army, and the local American Red Cross chapter gain currency from peer-to-peer solicitations and community pressure. Over time, contributions to charity come to be seen as something expected of businesses, small and large.

But small and midsize firms can also move from thinking of charitable contributions as obligations, as a form of societal dues, to viewing them as business opportunities. Creativity and generosity ascend as philanthropy is extended from an expression of altruistic impulse to a form of enlightened self-interest, one that motivates employees, enhances brand image, engages customers, and garners goodwill.

Indeed, hard evidence is accumulating that companies expressing concern through positive action about the health of communities in which they do business will be rewarded with superior performance.[6] Dover Management, which runs a mutual fund that invests in companies known for charitable giving, has shown that companies "with a good relationship between philanthropy and operating earnings have out-performed the S&P 500 by 3.5 percentage points a year over a five-year period."

Dover's research was confirmed by Professors Baruch Lev and Christine Petrovits of the New York University School of Business and Suresh Radhakrishnan of the University of Texas at Dallas School of Management. They concluded that for corporations, "doing good is apparently good for you." They found that "corporate charitable contributions are [particularly] effective in enhancing revenue in 'consumer sectors,' such as retailers and financial services."[7]

There is no reason to believe that similar advantages fail to accrue to small and midsize firms involved in philanthropy in highly attractive and visible ways.

THE LINCOLN CENTER EXPERIENCE

At Lincoln Center, we work hard to enjoy the best of both worlds. We appeal with success to large companies and greatly benefit from the Altria Group, Inc., American Express*, Bank of America Corporation, The Bank of New York Mellon Corporation*, Bloomberg L.P., Hearst Corporation*, Hess Corporation*, McKinsey & Company, Metropolitan Life Insurance Company, JPMorgan Chase & Co.*, Movado Group, Inc.*, Omnicom Group Inc.*, PepsiCo, Inc.*, Pfizer, Inc., RR Donnelley & Sons Company, Time Warner Inc., and The Walt Disney Company* as major corporate sponsors. Those asterisked companies are also generous donors to Lincoln Center's capital campaign. In addition, other firms have contributed $1 million to $5 million to our current capital campaign that are not corporate sponsors: American International Group, Inc., Citigroup, Inc., Credit Suisse Group, Deutsche Bank Group, The Goldman Sachs Group, Inc., Lehman Brothers, Inc., Macy's, Inc., Merrill Lynch & Co., Inc., Turner Construction Company, and UBS AG.

Appendix I amply documents the experience of Lincoln Center in raising annual support at a compound annual rate of 10.2 percent while simultaneously raising some $600 million for its capital campaign. Although many of the gifts in this total are large and significant, we were also bound and determined not to neglect small and medium-size businesses, particularly from among our geographic neighbors.

Our challenge was to conceive of a strategy and a compelling rationale that could embrace a special drive to woo local retailers, restauranteurs, cooperatives, condominiums, and rental buildings to our side.

That test of our imagination gave rise to the concept of a Lincoln Center Conservancy.

In essence, we argued that on May 11, 2009, Lincoln Center would be celebrating the fiftieth anniversary of its founding, dating back to 1959, when then President Eisenhower placed a shovel in the ground of a slum area on the West Side of Manhattan, the very site where the movie *West Side Story* was filmed.

When the New York Philharmonic and the Metropolitan Opera decided to move to this new and dangerous area of town, few would have guessed that in two generations it would become the wealthiest residential and commercial area in all of New York City. The Time Warner Center built but five blocks from Lincoln Center and the Hearst Building erected six blocks away are the most expensive pieces of commercial real estate in our city. Concurrently, a new residential tower, 15 Central Park West, only four blocks from our 16-acre campus, joined the adjacent Trump residences and Time Warner condominiums as the most costly residential spaces in a real-estate market already on high-price steroids.

And everyone I met—small business owner, retailer, restauranteur, developer, and investor—attributed their success on the Upper West Side in no small measure to Lincoln Center's presence and impact. With 5,500 full-time-equivalent employee jobs, with ten performing arts companies and two educational institutions, the Juilliard School and the School of American Ballet, spending annually a collective total of $700 million, with 5 million annual visitors and 4 million ticket buyers, it is no surprise that Lincoln Center was reliably estimated to have a $1.4 to $1.7 billion favorable impact on the metropolitan area economy.

And now Lincoln Center was about to invest well over $1 billion into its physical plant for the welfare of the next generation of artists and audiences. Its new modernized and expanded artistic facilities, its improvements to all public spaces, its introduction of mini-parks, lawns, benches, walkways, diversified food service, and twenty-first-century technology onto its Wi-Fied property, all hold promise of attracting hundreds of thousands of additional visitors.

They will buy merchandise, rent or purchase property, use private and mass transportation, and patronize neighborhood restaurants, we contended.

So, why not solicit local businesses, developers, real estate brokers, and restauranteurs to become members of the Lincoln Center Conservancy and help us maintain a unique physical and artistic complex that had done so much to having them thrive financially?

When I posed this notion to members of the Lincoln Center board of directors, it was greeted skeptically. Since all of Lincoln Center's neighbors benefit from our presence, why wouldn't they choose to remain economic free riders rather than contribute annually to this new group? Beyond their skepticism, the Business Improvement District (BID) was not happy about an impending solicitation for the Conservancy. The BID's budget was composed of annual sums that came in the form of assessments, many of them from the same businesses I would be soliciting. And while I made clear that we would refuse to accept a gift if it diminished, let alone threatened to eliminate, participation in the BID, still its president resisted our move. Even my own staff was less than enthusiastic. Change does not come simply, particularly to those easily threatened or when an idea is not invented here, but there.

Initiating a new order of things is tough in an established institution. Active resistance is common and easier to overcome. But passive resistance—of the kind Mahatma Gandhi would have admired—is a specialty at complex places like Lincoln Center. If the Lincoln Center Conservancy was to be created, only its president could be the champion of the cause.

I decided to give the whole effort a try and to do so personally. I took advice from a legendary fundraiser, Naomi Levine, who spent her entire professional life helping to move New York University from a fair to middling institution of higher education into one of the most sought after by students and faculty in the world.

Remember her guidance:

You don't raise major gifts by postage stamps. You do it by shoe leather.

I traipsed up and down and across the Upper West Side.

What I discovered was that logic has its limits. The claims of philanthropy go as much to the heart as to the head. Economic free-rider arguments did not necessarily apply.

It turns out that a fair number of those I approached were themselves West Siders. They had witnessed the utter transformation for the better of the extended neighborhood, and they credited Lincoln Center as a cause. They would give to the Lincoln Center Conservancy because it was the right thing to do.

Others were and are its patrons. So are their parents, their children, and, more often than not, their employees. For them, giving to the Conservancy was an act almost of self-interest, supporting the very institutions that they themselves enjoyed and took great pride in.

It was as if both groups were saying to me "What in heaven's name took you so long to ask?"

Others were favorably disposed but quite interested in the benefits Lincoln Center would offer in exchange for Lincoln Center Conservancy contributions.

Acknowledgment on our Web sites. Prominent mention in our literature. Privileged access to our ticket concierge desk to acquire the best available seats for performances at Lincoln Center. A window sticker to announce to customers and suppliers that one was a proud Lincoln Center Conservancy member. Attendance for employees at dress rehearsals. These were among the perquisites offered. Other benefits were introduced or those mentioned magnified in response to conversations with owners and investors in local businesses and developers of commercial and residential real estate.

Our objective was to raise between $1 and $2 million annually on a recurring basis or the equivalent of income at 5 percent from a $20 to $40 million permanent endowment to help maintain a beautifully renovated campus. That is a very ambitious goal.

TAKE A WALK, READ WIDELY

Whether we totally succeed or not, I am utterly persuaded that every nonprofit CEO should exit his or her office and walk two miles east, north, south, and west to see the organization as others do. Elicit their point of view. Ask about forms of new or enhanced cooperation. Explore possibilities of mutual support.

Strengthening relations in the community, learning from one's neighbors, taking the time to meet and greet fellow citizens will not only yield forms of support, it will engender goodwill and positive feeling. In the ATM machine of life, such visits create deposits of high value. Rest assured, the time will come when withdrawals are needed. When that happens, will you have a sufficiently high balance in your institution's account to sustain them?

The Lincoln Center Conservancy drive and all of the conversations, handshakes, and bonding it required insured that our bank balance of trust and confidence among neighbors is healthy. There is not likely to be a run on Lincoln Center's account.

Beyond stating clearly the compelling merits of your case to a business prospect, small or large, you must understand how that firm operates and how its interests intersect with your own. That inquiry entails homework. Learning how specific companies view their future, their products and services, their organization and culture, and their leadership is critical to sustaining a meaningful dialogue.

In the bibliography, I outline recommended reading: newspapers, periodicals, and books. Together, they will provide an intellectual map that can give conversations you have at the chamber of commerce or Kiwanis Club meetings greater meaning.

Dipping into that literature regularly will win you respect as someone not confined by the payroll you are on or the organization you lead. It will leave the impression that you understand the value of business to society and that you respect the role of the private sector and of government. It will also inform your conversations with prospects and demonstrate that you took the time to learn what they are about.

THE FOUNDATION

In theory, private foundations are very attractive potential sources of grants to nonprofit institutions. In 2007, some 68,000 of them were in existence in America, controlling assets of about $600 billion and giving away some $38.5 billion.[8]

Most of these entities employ little or no staff, define their priorities relatively clearly and narrowly, and depend on worthy institutions to apply. The larger foundations, by contrast, often conduct themselves, for better or worse, as if they knew best how to solve problems and seize challenges. By developing new initiatives, and sometimes offering start-up capital for the creation of new institutions, staff in larger foundations render it difficult for nonprofits in fields of compatible interest to apply for support.

In his definitive account of the American foundation, Joel Fleishman, a fan of this grant-making instrument, acknowledges that arrogance, secrecy, insularity, fuzziness, and lack of transparency and accountability are hardly unknown among the 200 largest foundations in America.[9] Although the barriers to entry may be high, the resources these foundations control suggest that it is worth the effort to attempt to figure out eligibility criteria for grants, judge the chances for success, and actually converse with a philanthropic officer.

In doing so, keep your expectations realistic. The review process probably will be tedious and time consuming. Access to the decision makers is rare and unusual, particularly for newcomers.

But remember, the business of foundations is giving money away. Is there a stranger manner in which to earn a living than to be employed by one of these institutions for the sole purpose of disseminating gifts? Your attitude should be that you are there to help the weary, wary, and beleaguered foundation staffer. After all, his or her employment depends on supplicants. Foundations need applicants, as stores need customers. They are in business to entertain your proposals, however much in practice it may appear to be otherwise. Be positive. Be persistent. Stay the course.

Here, too, doing your homework matters. Have you conducted enough research to determine that the work of your organization fits the area(s) of interest and the eligibility guidelines of the target foundation? Have you prepared a brief letter of inquiry followed up by a phone call to determine whether the specific idea(s) for funding you would like to proffer are of current foundation interest? If you formally apply and are turned down, did you really endeavor to find out the whys and wherefores, not in order to lodge a protest but to learn how to improve? And if you are fortunate enough to win a gift, do you treat the foundation as a friend and ally and ask how it can help you rally other funding sources to your side?

Although winning grants from foundations can be a frustrating process, in my experience too many fundraisers assume that declinations come from not being "insiders," from being insufficiently "cozy" with staff or trustees. Such an assumption removes responsibility from the solicitor and leads to an unproductive (and often unjustified) sense of cynicism.

Getting to know key foundation officials takes time. Do not fail to send literature about your place even when you are not asking for a grant. And by all means, invite foundation officials to visit your site at their convenience when something special is transpiring. Foundation fundraising is not for summer soldiers and sunshine patriots. Learning what your opposite number values in a nonprofit's proposal and performance will help you prepare a solicitation custom made for that foundation. Stay determined.

Do not underestimate how much merit matters. On the other side of the table are generally people of intelligence and goodwill, trying to dispense philanthropy in the most advantageous way with the highest impact on the problem being addressed.

Show them that the organization you represent fits that bill. The effort is bound to be rewarded, if not in every case, then in many.

CHAPTER 5

TECHNIQUE: SPECIAL EVENTS AND DIRECT MAIL

One gives generously and ends with more. Another stints on doing right and incurs a loss.

—Anonymous

You cannot win if you're not at the table. You have to be where the action is.

—Ben Stein

Woven into the exposition on how best to solicit individual donors, foundations, and corporations have been some key methods and skills:

- The essence of excellent oral and written communication.

- The routines of constant, attentive, and extensive reading and painstaking research.

- The art of writing a first-class funding proposal and a knock your-socks off, close-the-deal fundraising letter to major gift prospects.

Here I select two important ways and means of raising money, special events and direct mail. Both draw heavily on my personal experience. These methods of raising money require lots of attention to detail. Execution and customer focus really matter.

Craft a truly memorable special event or draft a direct mail piece that rivets the reader, and you accomplish much more than attracting new and existing donors through these special techniques. You broaden the base of contributors, many of whom are likely to become among your more generous and stalwart benefactors.

Call the process donor cultivation or climbing the ladder of fundraising, as you wish. Done well, special events and direct mail are indispensable methods of building a world-class philanthropic program of which you can be proud.

SPECIAL EVENTS

Fundraising events like galas, breakfasts, lunches, and dinners are a source of fuel for charities. Donors are publicly thanked. Adult men and women have an excuse to wear those new cuff links and display that new gown. To see and be seen doing some good is a form of public recognition most people cherish. Don't let them tell you otherwise. It isn't so.

Few activities in life are more fun than conceiving and executing a superb benefit or gala for your organization.

Identify a worthy honoree, someone, it is hoped, who is popular and not averse to asking for support.

With his or her help, choose cochairs who will do the heavy lifting on solicitations.

After figuring out the table and ticket pricing structure, presolicit, face to face, the highest category of supporters. At this level of asks, the chief executive should be personally involved.

At Lincoln Center, I introduced the $100,000 table and the $5 million gala. Underwriters at such an exalted level of giving must be seen face to face. They have a right to expect personal treatment and to be thanked early and often.

We also presolicit as many $50,000 and $25,000 tables as possible. Doing so makes having others sign on a lot easier. Gala attendees are as interested in who will be present as they are in the organization they are supporting and what will be performed. The more recognizable names commanding tables at higher prices, the better.

When mailing solicitations to trustees and requesting gala support, always sign the letter personally and always include a personal post-script carrying a pithy appeal. The latter should indicate that even if the occasion is impossible or inconvenient to schedule, a financial contribution to the success of the event would be warmly welcomed. Be sure the reply device includes a contribution line that's clearly delineated and easy to complete.

It is not uncommon for up to 20 percent of the gross proceeds of a gala to come from those who were unable to be physically present. Calendar conflicts are only an excuse for the failure to contribute, if you refrain from explicitly asking for support in lieu of attendance. Don't be shy.

Involve event leadership in the details of hall decoration, table settings, menu service, and the like. In cities like New York, nights out on the town on behalf of charity are frequent. Therefore, there is a premium on the new, the different, and the surprising. From the choice of speakers to the content of their remarks, from the quality of the printed program to what is in that take home gift bag, and from the warm greeting of all guests to the way in which thanks and appreciation are expressed—all of this and more can be memorable rather than humdrum and fun instead of tedious.

Remember, as useful as the event itself may be, and as helpful as the funds it raises, the real payoff resides in the opportunity to establish or solidify relationships with your organization. Approach every special event as a means to that end as well as an essential end in itself.

Importantly, it is often easier to solicit a corporation to purchase a table than to offer a grant or establish a partnership. If your nonprofit is honoring a leading customer of a firm or a sister organization in the same industry, a special event contribution is highly likely. What's more, funds for such occasions can be located throughout most firms, tucked away in advertising, human resource, and customer entertainment budgets. What better way to introduce your nonprofit to a company than to have some of its senior executives at an event where you control your message and show off your institution to best advantage?

Partying at Lincoln Center

Two examples from Lincoln Center may suffice to demonstrate the point.

Part of the $1 billion–plus physical transformation of Lincoln Center involved the top-to-bottom, inside-and-out renovation of Alice Tully Hall. Toward that end, the space was to be closed for at least 18 months. Rather than allow it to shut down unceremoniously, we decided to celebrate its temporary closure with a gala fundraiser.

We called it "Good Night Alice." We devised a program that reflected in microcosm Alice Tully Hall's past and promise. We televised it nationally on PBS stations as part of the series *Live From Lincoln Center*, now 32 years old. During the program, precious footage of the history of Lincoln Center and computerized renderings of its redevelopment were displayed for the first time to a national audience.

We were determined to impress even the most weary, wary, and naysaying guest. This would be a night to remember. You could tell by the Save the Date notice. It was a cardboard box, into which was nestled a facsimile pillow and a real mint with the words "Good Night Alice" and the date affixed to an inside flap. I know you are curious. Yes, it was dark chocolate. And, yes, the confections were an in-kind donation.

But that Save the Date was only the beginning of the sense that "Good Night Alice" would be a gala to remember.

First, we asked that no one wear black tie, and we started early so as to allow guests to be home no later than 11:00 P.M.

Second, because the performance was the last one to occur in Alice Tully Hall before renovation was to begin the next morning, guests were invited to bring their wine, martinis, water, and canapés into the auditorium, a once-in-a-lifetime treat.

Third, the evening's program on the stage of Alice Tully Hall was very special. It consisted of a mix of pieces and personalities that reflected in microcosm the past and future of this storied auditorium. Composers? Bernstein. Messiaen. Mendelssohn. Hermann. Glass. Anderson. Mozart. Noble. Adam Guettel. Performers? Philip Glass. Laurie Anderson. Wynton Marsalis. Kelli O'Hara. Ensembles? The principal players of the Chamber Music Society of Lincoln Center and the Juilliard Orchestra, 55 members strong, conducted by David Robertson. All of this and selected pieces of film about the history and future of Lincoln Center were narrated by Tom Brokaw, who served as host and, later, dinner honoree.

Fourth, when the performance ended, guests were escorted across the Lincoln Center campus toward a huge tent for dinner and celebratory activity. However, before entering, all gathered outdoors on a balmy April Monday evening with a new drink in hand supplied by strolling waiters to watch a surprise display of fireworks sparkling above Avery Fisher Hall. Mayor Bloomberg joined Lincoln Center's chairman, Frank Bennack, in calling the ten . . . nine . . . eight . . . seven . . . six . . . countdown that resulted in a gorgeously decorated sky.

Fifth, the tent! It was transformed into a make-believe construction site. On each table sat large toy centerpieces—cranes, derricks, large earth-moving trucks, outdoor elevators—that guests could take home. Before them was a tablecloth composed of construction drawings. On each table setting was placed a personally named lunchbox containing the appetizer. Drinks were served all night out of construction-worker thermoses.

The main course was served buffet style from chow trucks situated throughout the tent. Dessert consisted of vanilla ice cream and ten different kinds of nuts, syrups, creams, fruit, and other embellishments. Adults turned into kids as they prepared their own decadent sundaes!

At one end of the enormous tent was huge construction scaffolding from which music was played and speakers delivered their brief program.

Don't hesitate to use a gala to thank major donors, to regale the honoree with praise, and to state succinctly pertinent facts and observations about your cause. But don't overdo it. Oscar Wilde railed against those who believed that "nothing succeeds like excess." Every special event is a rare teachable moment to be exploited, but not at the expense of trying the patience of your audience. Remember the mantra for all speakers: "Be brief. Be engaging. Be sincere. Be seated."

As one departed the tent at evening's end, an invitation was tendered by a staff member to pick a take-home gift out of one of two large construction vehicles. Of course, everyone was also blessed with a personalized Lincoln Center construction hard hat. And all were warmly thanked for joining us.

These details and more—the wait staff in jeans, white shirts, and construction boots; the seating alternating with round and long tables—added up to a totally surprising, diverting, festive, one-of-a-kind, knockout evening.

Five and a half million dollars was raised that night. No one present will soon forget the event or, more important, what it celebrated: the launch of the most ambitious physical redevelopment of any performing arts center in the world.

As a result, four months later, members of the Lincoln Center's campaign leadership team were still arranging one-on-one major capital gift solicitation meetings with gala guests! The very kind of payoff one hopes for from a major special event.

Of course, none of this would be possible without energetic and imaginative as well as generous leadership. In this case, such qualities were packaged in a couple; Katherine Farley, a vice chair of Lincoln Center and chair of our Lincoln Center Development Project, and Jerry Speyer, the CEO of Tishman Speyer and a civic leader par excellence, now, among his many other involvements, the chairman of the board of the Museum of Modern Art.

Indispensable, as well, is a very talented special events staff headed by Tamar Podell and her colleagues Mary Callaghan and Barbara Bell Cook. The extended team they brought together including the designer of the event and the caterer, Restaurant Associates, delivered a high-quality result.

Well, it is unseemly to say good-bye to Alice and not welcome her back when the new resplendent hall is ready for a sneak preview. As I write, preparations are well under way for a "Welcome Back Alice" event to take place in February 2009. But even before, in the run-up to Lincoln Center's fiftieth anniversary, we plan to open the hall on December 8, 2008, only to invited guests.

Called "50 by 50 for 50," the idea is that no fewer than 50 benefactors will host dinners in their homes to celebrate the hall's completion and Lincoln Center's fiftieth birthday. Each host agrees to donate an incremental $50,000 and to pay for the full cost of dinner. After dinner, all guests are invited to the first (private) event ever held in the new Alice Tully Hall, a concert by the singer Michael Feinstein.

Economically, with 50 hosts pledging $50,000 ($2.5 million), with JPMorgan Chase & Co. as corporate underwriter for the event (pledging $350,000), with guests bound to demonstrate thanks to hosts with their own gifts to Lincoln Center, and with yet another opportunity to sell named seats in the new hall at $5,000 and $10,000 each, we hope for a result approaching $5 million. And, of course, if we execute "50 by 50 for 50" memorably, awareness of redevelopment will widen and deepen and new prospects for major capital gifts will arise, some through thoughtful planning and plotting and some serendipitously.

Putting It Together, Bit by Bit

With so much at stake, scrupulous attention to event details is simply critical.

Will the caterer be prepared for the vegetarians, or those who keep kosher or halal diets, thereby communicating how much Lincoln Center welcomes and accommodates all?

Will extra staff be assigned to coat checking during cold or inclement weather, thereby avoiding the tediousness of long lines on entry or exit?

Will there be projection screens around the hall or multiple podiums, thereby assuring that there is no best seat or best table?

Will food be pretasted, acoustics prechecked, and calls to chairs and honorees placed to insure that all is properly arranged and all of the evening's key players are comfortable?

Will carefully composed thank-you messages be emailed and sent by letter the very next day to honorees and all major benefactors as well as to key staff responsible for the event's success?

Lincoln Center strives to have its special events as carefully produced and delivered as is the activity celebrated on its legendary stages. Doing so contributes to a reputation for quality and caring that guests tend not to forget.

Benefits Pay

In a typical year, all told, Lincoln Center will hold no fewer than ten galas that range in size from 250 to 1,200 guests and in gross proceeds from $250,000 to $5.5 million. They are critical to all aspects of our fundraising operation.

One of the vital assets that Lincoln Center enjoys from a fundraising perspective is that we can bring existing and prospective donors to witness and enjoy precisely what we do. Another is that we can place those real and aspiring benefactors in the company of others. For hours at a time, they are a captive audience to whom we can deliver a memorable evening filled with positive messages.

That is why we hold a fundraiser each January to benefit our American Songbook series when supposedly all wealthy New Yorkers are in Palm Beach, Palm Springs, or the Caribbean. Not so.

It is why we tailor a special event for the hedge fund community with an accent on informality and networking. There is no fixed table seating, just food stations and bars that allow guests to migrate around an attractively decorated room. Our entertainment also reflects the audience. For what other event would we ask Jon Stewart or Stephen Colbert to be hosts? Where else would we insist on 60-minute, intermissionless performances of the likes of Diana Krall or the Wallflowers, a rock band led by Bob Dylan's son Jakob?

Our hedge fund and private equity guests have limited attention spans and BlackBerry addictions. We need to present just enough to engage them but never to edge close to boring them. We seek a Goldilocks event.

And beyond our more traditional seated dinner (black tie or otherwise) preceding an orchestral concert or solo recitalist offered in the spring and fall, we also devote one December afternoon to a family festival.

It consists of lunch for kids and their parents or grandparents. Stilt walkers. Clowns. Cookie decorators. Portrait artists. Karaoke recording machines. Makeup artists. Mimes. Photographers everywhere. And enough candy to make deliriously happy all of the dentists in Manhattan!

Then, after lunch, guests have their choice of performances to attend together. The New York City Ballet performing *The Nutcracker*. A show brought to us by the Big Apple Circus. A movie in the Walter Reade Theater especially chosen for the occasion by the experts at the Lincoln Center Film Society. The amazing Rob Kapilow displaying his brilliant lecture/demonstration techniques about classical music especially for children.

Where else but at Lincoln Center would so many attractive offerings be available to kids just steps away from one another, all within walking distance?

When I was serving as the president of the International Rescue Committee (IRC), one of our major fundraising challenges derived from the physical and psychic distance of the donor or prospective benefactor from the condition of the refugee or displaced person.

We could communicate in writing about the experience of our needy refugees, 80 percent of whom are women and children. We could invite guests to listen to our expatriate and international staff describe their experiences at brown-bag lunches or parlor meetings. We could use our annual fundraiser to videotape images about the IRC's work and introduce the audience to a refugee or two who would tell their own stories, even in a setting as auspicious as the Waldorf-Astoria Grand Ballroom. And of course we could ask donors to accompany us on site visits to our field locations around the world, uncomfortable, inconvenient, and difficult as those outings might be.

All of this and more was taken on with energy and determination. Alas, the number of people we could reach through such methods was measured in the hundreds each year and fell far short of our ambition.

By contrast, at Lincoln Center, the obstacles to existing donors are few, far between, and mostly self-induced. All that stands between exposing interested parties to our work and superb results is our imagination, energy, creativity, and resourcefulness.

We warm to the challenge. In 2002, when I arrived at Lincoln Center, there were a total of five special events yielding $3.3 million in gross revenue. In 2007, we held ten special events, yielding almost five times the gross revenue, $15.7 million. The fundraising dividends that have resulted from relationships struck and strengthened with donors of all stripes are simply incalculable.

DIRECT MAIL FUNDRAISING

Everyone is a potential donor. The limits on fundraising are less the resources or willingness of donors than the energy, imagination, or drive of fundraisers. The most far-reaching and egalitarian form of fundraising is direct mail (often combined with telemarketing).

In any piece of direct mail, the objective must be to break through the clutter of the recipient's life and rivet his or her attention.

Whether you are attempting to acquire a new donor or a renewal (and, it is hoped, an upgrade) of a current one, here are seven key questions to address:

1. Is your mailing being sent to the correct prospects, whether the list is owned in-house, rented, bartered, or purchased from others?

2. Are you mailing at the right time of year, when recipients are most likely to pay some attention to the appeal?

3. Have you given adequate thought to the animating message of the piece, to its author, to its "look," and to the content of the ask?

4. Has consideration been given to utilizing "star power" names aligned to your cause that will attract attention and to the appeal of the offer, from the donor benefits listed to the possibility that gifts received by a given deadline will be matched by a named (or anonymous) donor?

5. Is there a follow-on mailing planned and/or outbound telephone marketing follow-up?

6. Have your acquisition and/or gift renewal mailings been adequately pretested with sample audiences?

7. Nothing happens unless an envelope is opened. What is on the outside of yours that will entice the recipient to unseal it rather than throw it away?

A piece of direct mail should be a call to action. Stimulating positive behavior is what a successful campaign is all about.

At the IRC, we enjoyed considerable success by associating well-known, credible, reliable personalities with our ask.

One example is Andy Grove, the former CEO and cofounder of Intel, a refugee who escaped from Budapest to freedom in Vienna during the

Hungarian Revolution of 1956. Because Andy is so widely admired in business circles and because he had just been named the *Time Magazine* Person of the Year for 1998, we decided to ask him to sign an appeal letter. It began in this arresting way.

Dear Friend:

My name is Andy Grove.

I am a refugee.

By telling succinctly and powerfully how the IRC came to his rescue and about how many hundreds of thousands of others it could assist with the reader's help, Andy's letter broke all records in terms of favorable replies.

The IRC was fortunate as well to win Paul Newman's approval to have mailings go out over his signature. Here the personal connection with the organization was less direct and compelling. But Newman's high name recognition and his attractiveness as a generous donor to many causes, including the IRC, proved to be very successful.

For almost two decades, Paul Newman has devoted all of the profits from his burgeoning wholesale food enterprise—from "Newman's Own" sauces, popcorn, salad dressing, lemonade, cookies, and the like—to worthy institutions and causes. That the IRC was among them and singled out for praise in Newman's appeal letter made for a winner.

Another personality-driven appeal came from Tom Brokaw. His 17 years as NBC's news anchor won him extraordinarily high name recognition and credibility. His connections with the IRC were wide and deep. One of his children was employed by the agency for a time. Another volunteered for it. Tom himself officiated for a decade at the IRC's annual gala. He continues to do so. And Tom actually became cochair of the IRC's board of overseers.

These connections enabled him to write with authenticity and authority on the IRC's merits and of its needs.

The results have been spectacular.

For smaller organizations that are regionally or community based, a local figure well known in the community could work just as well as a prominent national "star."

But solid direct mail financial returns are not necessarily dependent on who signs the letter. The cause itself—compellingly stated—can carry the day. At the IRC, we struggled with how best to capture the terrifying plight of people suddenly displaced from their homes, lacking their possessions, even their identity papers, with no place to go. Stressing the drama of how the IRC came to the emergency assistance of those who flee in fear of persecution was our constant challenge. And demonstrating that the IRC is extraordinarily efficient and effective, spending less than 10 percent of its funds on what might be called "overhead" or "management and general," was an important attribute worth stressing.

The IRC's provision of water and sanitation, of medical care, of security protection, of reuniting young separated children and their families truly saves lives. Thousands of them. How best to portray the drama and impact of the IRC's benevolent intervention?

Staff crafted a letter called "Thirty Minutes to Pack." It asked the reader to fully identify with the plight of a victim. How would you gather your family? What possessions would you take? Where would you go, and how would you get there?

It began in this utterly riveting way.

> You have 30 minutes to pack everything you own. If you and your family can't carry it on your backs, it will have to stay behind. Look around one last time because you may never return to this home again. And, be careful what route you take. Choose wrong and your family could perish by nightfall . . .

Versions of this piece were used to take advantage of the public's focus on so many crises: Rwanda, Bosnia, Kosovo, East Timor, the Eastern Congo. Indeed, this theme has proven to be among the most successful in drawing positive returns.

In Appendix IV you will find the three most successful direct mail fundraising letters ever sent by the IRC over the signatures of Messrs. Newman, Brokaw, and Levy, respectively. You will notice virtually no mention of benefits to the donor. Such benefits are viewed as almost incompatible with the humanitarian mission. By comparison, a typical Lincoln Center mailing is strewn with references to how tax-deductible donations are fully compatible with enjoying the privileges of insider access to special events, to priority ticket services, and to discounts.

There are many variations on these basic guidelines. But be warned: Direct mail is an expensive form of fundraising. Telemarketing, even more so. It requires a multiyear effort and a level of substantial investment, with little or no net positive return, for at least three or four major campaigns.

Judging where to put your scarce fundraising resources is a major strategic question. Are opportunities more attractive in pursuing government sources of funding, or foundation, corporation, and major individual gifts? Are benefits and special events likely to yield a more robust return than direct mail solicitations?

Whether and how much to invest in which forms of fundraising requires sober financial analysis.

Grappling with finite resources, nonprofit institutions are constantly confronted with the necessity for choice. It is the task of leadership to choose wisely and well.

CHAPTER 6

TOUGH QUESTIONS: CANDID ANSWERS

You may say I'm a dreamer, but I'm not the only one.

—John Lennon

Anything not worth doing well is not worth doing.

—Warren Buffett

In our day-to-day working lives, I am struck by how many government agencies, businesses, and nonprofit institutions actively discourage learning on the job. To ask a question is not to express a curiosity or demonstrate an eagerness to grow. Rather, posing an inquiry exposes a vulnerability, uncovers a weakness.

Too often, one must leave the office to learn, unobserved, rather than run the risk of revealing ignorance to one's colleagues.

The Supreme Court Justice Oliver Wendell Holmes once observed that "in the life of the law an ounce of experience is worth a pound of logic." The same is true of fundraising. And because so much of fundraising is private, the chance to compare notes and learn from the successes and failures of others is very limited.

In recognition of how difficult it may be to have one's fundraising questions answered with candor, I have collected some of the most challenging questions I have ever been asked. They are articulated in this chapter, together with my considered responses.

In *Yours for the Asking*, learning is all about gain, not pain. Painless learning should permeate all workplaces, where those who strive to improve are encouraged, not derided, and where everyone acknowledges that excellent performance is the product of a process of continuous improvement.

EMERGING NONPROFITS: NEWER, SMALLER

Apart from your service as staff director of the Task Force on the New York City Fiscal Crisis and executive director of the 92nd Y, you've tended to lead pretty large nonprofit organizations, like the International Rescue Committee and Lincoln Center. How would you adjust the advice dispensed in *Yours for the Asking* to fit smaller and newer nonprofits?

Substantial parts of this book are applicable to all nonprofits, large, medium size, and small and in whatever field they may operate.

Raising funds from individuals, foundations, and corporations does not change very much based on the size of your organization.

What is different are the assets each nonprofit brings to a fundraising appeal. How extensive is your impact in terms of population served, directly or indirectly? How does your nonprofit's distinctive approach to providing services compensate for the modest numbers of favorably affected clients, students, patients or audience members?

Younger and smaller organizations are often compelled to choose their fundraising targets and methods more carefully. The size of their paid staff does not allow for a broad-based, diversified approach.

For example, some nonprofits may simply and wisely concede that apart from small businesses, corporate philanthropy and sponsorship is highly unlikely.

Others may acknowledge that while a larger, wealthier, and better connected board would be nice, it is not likely to happen in the near term. That process will take longer than would be the case with an older, more established, and better-known organization.

What is different is access to influential donors. The newer, the smaller, the less sophisticated will have limited success, early on.

What's important is that each institution play to its strengths. Don't focus on organizational attributes you wish were real. Win the fundraising battles with the weapons at your disposal. Or, as President Teddy Roosevelt famously advised: "Do what you can, with what you have, where you are."

For example, if I were the executive director of a community-based museum in the Bronx, I would accentuate the favorable impact of my institution on my borough—on community service, on educational impact, on economic development, and on civic pride.

I would highlight the number of volunteers attracted to my nonprofit and the support I enjoy from partnerships with organized labor, nearby housing projects, community centers, houses of worship, and elementary and secondary schools. I would look to my borough president, City Council member, mayor, state assemblyman, and state senator as well as my congressman to support the museum with relevant city, state, and federal funding.

I would emphasize my relatively low overhead and my relatively high "sweat equity" from volunteers.

I would approach foundations oriented to the working class, to the disadvantaged, to the underdog, and to the "outer boroughs."

I would prowl my extended neighborhood looking for small businesses and branch offices of large firms like banks, telephone equipment companies, and retail chains and seek their help.

I would research the names of the now-affluent born and raised near the museum or in the borough of the Bronx and appeal to those who have made it not to forget where they came from. Give something to the place that nurtured you and help those left behind you to climb the ladder of success you have enjoyed, I would implore.

It is a lot tougher to raise private funds when you are smaller, newer, and less sophisticated about the ways of Wall Street than of Main Street. But do not underestimate what applied common sense, highly motivated volunteers, and the enthusiasm of professionals blissfully unaware of what they supposedly cannot accomplish will do for strengthening your fundraising results, year after year.

Rome was not built in a single day. Fundraising is a marathon, not a sprint.

THE PHILANTHROPIC POSTMORTEM: CRITIQUING PERFORMANCE

How would you recommend that development staffs critique their own performance with a view toward continuous improvement?

It is extremely important for fundraising professionals to review their work in a thorough, uninhibited, and disciplined manner.

There are at least four ways to assess progress and maintain an active performance scorecard. They can best be expressed in the form of an equal number of questions:

1. Did our fundraising in the last fiscal year overall, by market segment (corporations, small businesses, large foundations, family foundations, individual major gifts, and modest gifts) and by method (face-to-face solicitations, written proposal, special event, direct mail, testamentary giving) meet, beat, or fall short of budgeted expectations?

2. Was our fundraising in the last fiscal year a measurable improvement over the prior year's results?

3. How does our fundraising track record compare with other admired institutions, overall, by market segment and by method?

4. Are we successfully bridging the gap between our fundraising promise and performance, year over year?

The first question requires a detailed analysis of actual experience versus budget, together with explanations for shortfalls and performance exceeding expectations. Understanding how we have fared and why enables us to reach sound decisions about the allocation of fundraising resources; about the adequacy of existing staff and their needs for training, reward, and recognition; and about what targets should be set for next year's budget and why.

The second question allows one to appraise progress in an evolutionary way. Were our efforts to improve performance by segment and method from one fiscal year to the next successful? If so, how so? If not, why?

The third question compels us to look outside the confines of our own shop and inquire after how our colleagues tackle similar challenges, overall, by segment and by method. What can we learn from them that is adaptable to our own environment? How, precisely, did they achieve superior performance, and what will it take for us to meet or exceed their results?

At Lincoln Center, we frequently check out how Columbia and New York universities, the Brooklyn Academy of Music, the New York Public Library, the Museum of Natural History, the Museum of Modern Art, the Metropolitan Museum of Art, among others, conceive and conduct their programs. To be sure, our institution is different in mission, history, and culture. Few initiatives or practices are easily transferable in their current form from one organization to another. Nonetheless, how others fare and why are lessons that can help improve the means and the ends of Lincoln Center's development efforts.

The fourth question is the most challenging and tantalizing. It asks us to compare ourselves not to our budget, nor to prior-year performance, nor even to the conduct of others. Rather, it beseeches us to strive for an ideal, to dream grandly of how well we would perform if we broke the existing mold, engaged in disruptive thinking and raised our fundraising game to peerless, world-class performance.

By keeping in mind these four questions and consistently testing ourselves against them, by doing so in an uninhibited way with our defenses down and our curiosity and learning antennas up, we help to create a

work environment where learning from one another, teamwork, and the
highest quality of professionalism are prized and richly rewarded.

As we do so, gaps in knowledge are uncovered, the need to strength-
en core competencies revealed, and the adequacy of current staff capacity and performance better understood. With such conclusions
drawn, it is now possible to craft remedial hiring, training, measure-
ment, and educational initiatives to bridge these identified gaps.

FUNDRAISING IN STORMY WEATHER

What accounts for your optimism about the potential for unprecedented gains
in fundraising? After all, by the end of May 2008, the stock market was moving
sideways and the NASDAQ, S&P, and Dow were well beneath their historic
highs. The level of unemployment grew to exceed 5 percent while job creation
slowed to a halt. Oil prices spiked to over $140 a barrel. The housing crisis
deepened (foreclosures ominously high, prices continuing to plummet), and
consumer purchasing power weakened further with each passing month. Given
these signs of existing or forthcoming recession, is the outlook for increased
philanthropy realistic?

I write during a heated presidential primary season. What had been
expected to be a campaign dominated by foreign policy, in general, and
the Iraq war, in particular, has instead been overshadowed by health
policy, immigration policy, and concerns about the domestic economy.

The subprime mortgage crisis and the ensuing resignations in rapid
succession of Charles Prince as chief executive of Citi Inc., Stanley
O'Neal as CEO of Merrill Lynch, James Cayne as CEO of Bear Stearns,
Marcel Ospel as CEO of UBS, and G. Kennedy Thompson as CEO of
Wachovia due to tens of billions of dollars of losses and writedowns for
these firms were shocking. Other institutions, such as Morgan Stanley,
Deutsche Bank, Credit Suisse, and Bank of America, also found them-
selves caught in risk management crises of significant proportions.

All of this shook the confidence of financial markets. Moreover,
the weekend intervention of the Federal Reserve Bank on March 15

and 16, 2008, to arrange for JPMorgan Chase and Co.'s secured take-over of Bear Stearns caused, in a flash, the disappearance of a venerable investment house otherwise bound for bankruptcy. Gloom spread as it became clear that the real economy was also suffering from the blows of higher commodity prices, housing foreclosures, construction slow-downs, less consumer purchasing power, and the like.

There may be cause for some psychological gloom. There is no reason for any impending sense of doom.

First of all, since Jimmy Carter's presidency, recessions have been few and far between. They have been shallow and they have been short. There is little reason to believe that the economic sluggishness now being experienced will differ materially this time around in length or depth.

Second, while some of the wealthy may use the economic and stock market correction as an excuse not to give or to give less, the truth is that the affluent donate much more from their assets than their income. Fear not, the fortunate are generally well protected against the vicissitudes of a modest recession. Their philanthropy should be virtually unaffected.

Third, looked at historically, there has been no five-year period in which philanthropy has failed to grow in excess of inflation from 1977 through 2006. A slowdown, yes. An occasional and very brief down-turn for individuals if take-home pay is adversely affected, for founda tions if stock market returns are discouraging, and for corporations if earnings plummet. But not much more than a slackening.

The naysayers, the skeptics, and the Cassandras will have a field day predicting harsh results. Neither history, nor the tremendous gains in net assets in the last decade and a half, nor the pattern of corporate earnings growth suggests a cause for alarm.

Fundraisers who worry aloud excessively should be aware of the im-pact of the self-fulfilling prophesy. Nothing in the economy, even short term, cannot be rectified by more energetic, intelligent, and resourceful asking.

Indeed, by casting your fundraising net broader and into deeper waters, the "catch" will not only surprise you, it will help cushion the blow from downturns in segments of the economy.

Are you endeavoring to attract donors from outside your immediate geographic area of service, here in the United States or overseas?

Are you increasing the reach and the return of special events, direct mail, and e-philanthropy?

Are bequests receiving the attention they deserve?

Do you view transitions in the leadership of corporations and private foundations as opportunities to build on prior success or to introduce your institution or cause as if for the first time to fresh eyes and more open, eager ears?

Is there room to enlarge your board of directors and raise the expectations of its members for giving and getting?

By adopting these and other measures, by broadening and diversifying your sources of support, American recessions will be more irritants and challenges than determinants of your fundraising fate.

FUNDRAISING: WHO IS IN CHARGE AND WHEN

What is the real value added offered by a CEO to an institution's fundraising capability? And how does it feel to be in charge of securing the resources necessary to balance budgets, to finance special projects and to bring capital campaigns to a successful conclusion?

I would posit that the larger the nonprofit organization, the less a CEO can measurably and substantially improve fundraising performance.

The huge state and private universities and the long-standing liberal arts colleges enjoy tens of thousands of loyal alumni and alumnae, most grateful for their fine educations, and many still eager to curry favor with the powers that be for the admission of their own children. They are indulged as well by an affluent parent body of existing students, captivated by the contemporary experience of their offspring and eager to help. And they benefit from a network of associations with leading corporations and foundations.

The nation's prestigious research and teaching hospitals encounter a world that sometimes seems divided between grateful former patients and those hoping for special treatment should they need specialized medical assistance. Both points of vantage often lead to generosity among donors.

Weighed against these major embedded advantages, can a CEO really matter? Arguably not. Unless . . .

Unless he or she sets forth an animating vision rendering the whole institution far more than the sum of its parts.

Unless he or she recruits an extraordinary cadre of professional managers and complements these gifted fundraising professionals with generous, talented, galvanized volunteers.

Unless he or she devotes extraordinary energy to having a felt presence all around the university or hospital and wherever graduates or former patients and their families reside.

Unless he or she sets goals that raise an institution's sights and stretch its capabilities.

Under such circumstances, a president truly can be said to add value.

Although the direct involvement of a CEO may be desirable at larger universities and hospitals, it is often not necessary.

The opposite is true at a smaller or newer nonprofit, or as in the case of Lincoln Center, where the goals set for fundraising are so large as to be unprecedented. In these cases, the president's fundraising role is simply indispensable. In these cases, the president is doing more than meeting a fundraising target, he or she is establishing a culture of asking and building a foundation on which future campaigns can rest.

Such presidents often feel weary and wary. "Heavy lies the head that wears the crown."

The sense of responsibility is profound. The demands on the CEO's time are relentless. But the rewards can be magnificent.

I vividly recall a visit to a displaced persons camp in rural Burundi, about 100 miles south of its capital, Bujumbura. The scene was horrific. No access to clean water. Children separated by civic strife from their parents. Ill fed. Ill clothed. Listless. I felt helpless and silly, having brought with me a soccer ball. These kids had no energy to walk, let alone play.

Their bodies were torn, bony, or bloated. Their heads afflicted with scabies. Their eyes calling out for help. The stench of ignored and emaciated dead bodies was all around us.

I left my IRC colleagues to their early work in this newly formed "settlement," bound and determined to do something about it.

When I landed at JFK airport, the nearest customs inspector ran the distinct risk of being solicited for the cause. While my better judgment had me leaving him alone, for the next week I did little but seek donations for these kids. Seared in my mind were the smells of a camp with no latrines and the sights of rampant disease. Well, seven days and $300,000 later, I wired that sum to my colleagues in Burundi.

And after only a month had transpired, after latrines had been built, a water well dug, new pipe laid to another water source, inoculations given to all of the children, and nutritious food delivered daily, the change was dramatic.

There on my computer were pictures of many of the same children I had observed but ten weeks before playing soccer and smiling with the joy of discovery.

How does it feel? Like you have been summoned to offer the gift of life. Like you are in a state of ecstasy.

FUNDRAISING MYTHS AND REALITIES

Every field of endeavor is filled with myths that mislead, confuse, and lead one astray. Choose two of your favorites and suggest how they are undermined by realities.

In fundraising, false choices are often put before us. We are challenged unnecessarily to choose between the methods by which we raise funds or between their sources. Often the key to success in any realm is to short-circuit bifurcated thinking, to declare "the end of either/or."

A recent example comes from Bill Gross, the billionaire guru at Pim-co, the bond firm owned by Allianz SE. He has seen the philanthropic light, and he is palpably angry at those who do not fully share his views. Here's Gross in uninhibited, raw prose.

> Trust funds, for the kids, inheritances for the grandkids, multiple vacation homes, private planes, multi-million-dollar birthday bashes and ego-rich donations to local art museums and concert halls are but a few of the ways rich people waste money—and I admit I am guilty of at least one of this admittedly short list of sins.

> I have, however, avoided the last one. When millions of people are dying from AIDS and malaria in Africa, it is hard to justify the umpteenth society gala held for the benefit of a performing arts center or an art museum. A thirty million dollar gift for a concert hall is not philanthropy, it is a Napoleonic coronation.[1]

Wondering what the views of Mr. Gross really are?

What is to be gained by pitting one cause against another? After all, the arts donor may or may not also give to humanitarian causes. Suggesting that failing to do so is as thoughtless and ego-gratifying as throwing egregious parties for oneself (is that the unidentified sin Gross is guilty of?) is nothing short of silly.

The quintessential value of philanthropy is choice, the freedom to give your own funds to institutions and causes you believe in. As the former president of the International Rescue Committee, I am in as good a position as anyone to be pleased that Gross is focused in his philanthropy on public health in Africa, however belatedly. But to belittle those who choose otherwise is to resurrect the myth of "either/or" and to do so in a way that attributes motives to donors quite unfairly.

It is also to ignore the role of governments, including the United States. The foreign assistance of nation-states given more generously in response to the demands of Mr. Gross as citizen will achieve much more than whistling into the winds of well-established philanthropy. Problems of the scale of AIDS, tuberculosis, and malaria

need public commitment and resources, not just more private charitable assistance.

Rwandans, Congolese, Sudanese, Somalis, and Ethiopians are
aware of the critical need to address public health crises as a high priority. They prefer that it be addressed by support from governments
and that they not be treated as "charity cases." But they are *also* very
proud of African indigenous music, visual art, theater, poetry, and
literature. To give up one cause for another is to deny one's heritage,
to choose foolishly, falsely, and unnecessarily. Not only in America,
but all around the world, the arts are the embodiment of universalistic
values and aspirations that merit exposure and matter deeply to proud
citizens.

Someone ought to introduce Gross to a museum containing African
visual art or sculpture or a performing arts center featuring African
music and dance. Perhaps it is not too late for him to see the wisdom of
the end of either/or. Lincoln Center would be pleased to be the locus
for a changed perspective.

The second favorite myth perpetuated both by alarmist fundraisers
and by a media unsophisticated in the ways of charity is "donor
fatigue." After Hurricane Katrina and the tsunami in 2004, it was
widely speculated that these causes had been so compelling for
donors as to crowd out other charitable drives from their consideration.[2]

Well, it turns out that for both victims of Katrina and of the tsunami,
an impressive total of $5 billion was donated. But that total is less
than 2 percent of all gifts to charity in 2004. There is just as much reason to believe that the outpouring of support to those adversely affected by natural disasters is supplemental to, rather than in lieu of,
other gifts.

Indeed, as in the case of 9/11 fundraising, what we are probably
witnessing is growing awareness of human needs generally. Natural
and man-made disasters are teachable moments. They are more likely
to stimulate new or supplemental interest in very well publicized cases
than they are to induce so-called donor fatigue.

A CEO'S TWO FRIENDS: THE WATCH AND THE LIST

How do you find ample time to raise funds as the chief executive officer of a nonprofit institution with many other responsibilities to shoulder, processes to manage, and results to pursue?

It is not easy. Fundraising demands stamina. Leading what is, in effect, a permanent campaign for your institution or cause requires determination, persistence, and lots of time.

The various sources of funding—individual and institutional—and the many methods of solicitation —face to face, written proposal, direct mail, bequest, and special event—each operate on its own calendars and rhythms.

On a well-functioning fundraising team, the chief executive is the quarterback. More often than not, the CEO is expected to set the game plan in the locker room, dictate tactics in the huddle, call the plays, and execute on the passing and the running game on the field.

Translated from football to development, the president is supposed to formulate strategy with volunteers and professional staff, lead most face-to-face solicitations, review written proposals, prepare voluminous correspondence, help to design special events, and mix and mingle at galas until a quarter to three, when there is no one in the place except me and my wife, Liz. These activities are punctuated by frequent meetings and phone calls throughout a typical workday.

Some prospects prefer breakfast, lunch, or dinner meetings. Some think holidays are a perfect time to gather with those representing a nonprofit. That prospect may need last-minute tickets to a sold-out event, or a restaurant reservation when all the tables are booked. He may need immediate access to a particular physician for a family member, or help in getting an elderly parent access to the right kind of nursing care. All of this activity absorbs energy. Fundraising is a client-focused journey. You must be present when the customer is available and willing, not at your convenience.

I have lost count of the vacations deferred or postponed and the time with my wife curtailed. Sleep deprivation, let's not go there.

If your goals are lofty, if the cause is noble, then the fundraising process is often relentless and the personal costs consequential.

I have always given raising funds from trustees, individuals, foundations, and corporations the highest priority. Internal processes and business can often wait. A prospective donor cannot be kept on hold.

My allies in this struggle to preserve as many hours as possible in every day and week to raise funds are the watch and the list.

I am a stickler for short, well-prepared, highly focused meetings. They are scheduled tightly, back to back, and I am devoted to having them start and end on time.

My deal with Lincoln Center's staff is this. My door is always open to you, as is my schedule. I will answer all emails, phone calls, and paper correspondence, with rare exception, on the day they are received. But if a donor prospect calls while we are meeting, I will interrupt our session to pick up the phone.

To an executive, time is a precious and perishable commodity. It can be either your enemy or your ally. By using parts of weekends, very early mornings, and very late evenings to catch up on paperwork, correspondence, and reading, the "normal" business day is freed up for internal meetings and for phone calls and management by walking around.

Your second friend is the list. Every day, I know precisely what I want to accomplish to move forward the institution I help lead. And every day, it is as if internal and external forces conspire to keep me from attending to the items on that list in favor of someone else's priorities. By being vigilant about inner direction and priority setting, one can process interruptions, satisfy the legitimate needs of others inside and outside of the organization, and still accomplish what you were bound and determined to do.

The hours are long. One boss told me I was a Jew who believed in the Protestant ethic. Another claimed that if I fell out of bed in the middle of the night, I would be entitled to worker's compensation, as the job was always on my mind.

It is a small price to pay when you see the results of your labor and that of your colleagues, doing what Aeschylus urged: "taming the savageness of man and making gentler the life of this world."

FOUR HALL OF FAME FUNDRAISERS: MY NOMINEES

You were privileged to work at the side of successful fundraisers. Please select a few and explain what about them was special in your experience.

Beverly Sills

When it comes to fundraising, and much else, Beverly Sills was one of a kind.

She served on the Search Committee that attracted me to Lincoln Center. I reported to her for six months before she left the post of chair of Lincoln Center after eight years of service.

In many ways, she was the ideal fundraiser.

Her stature as the world's leading soprano, her rags- (all right, working-class) to-riches story, and her extraordinary network of colleagues and friends meant that virtually no one would fail to return Beverly's phone call or refuse her an audience.

What other artist can you name who served on such corporate boards as Time Warner, American Express, and Human Genome Sciences?

Before the term *crossover artist* had been invented, Beverly Sills embodied its meaning. Can you identify a diva who regularly appeared on *The Tonight Show* with Johnny Carson (and guest hosted it), who did hour-long television specials with the likes of Carol Burnett, and whose on-camera close friends were the Muppets? It was no surprise that her name recognition throughout the United States and the world remained at stratospheric levels for decades.

Has there ever been an artistic figure as comfortable with elected and appointed officials—city, state and federal—as Beverly?

Her reach was simply staggering.

And, in her presence, the sense of humor, the poise, the persuasiveness, and the charm were entirely disarming. She knew why she was with you, and she was not leaving without a gift commitment. Her sheer energy and joy won you over. It was not for nothing that her nickname was Bubbles.

What is more, Beverly could take a staff briefing about a prospective donor she had never met and a description of a funding need only minutes before the encounter. Without a note in front of her, she delivered a pitch-perfect presentation that seemed untutored and effortless.

In Chapter 8, devoted to humor and fundraising, I cite several examples of Beverly's fundraising success. Her capacity to raise funds became almost as legendary as her artistic accomplishments after she retired as a singer at age 50. Her performance as an artist and as a solicitor was nothing short of breathtaking.

David Rubenstein

One of the most fascinating people I've encountered in my professional life is David Rubenstein, the founder of the Carlyle Group and a self-made billionaire.

To give you a flavor for the self-deprecating, self-effacing, modest nature of David, I will tell a tale not out of school but out of the Grand Tier dining room of the Metropolitan Opera House.

David was dining with me and my wife, Elizabeth, and with Gail and Carl Icahn. Carl was describing to us his views of Time Warner Inc., a firm with which he was then publicly tangling. At one point he stopped suddenly and asked David: "And how about you?"

"Well, actually, I began my professional life as a lawyer. That didn't work very well.

"Then I went to work for a president who gave the country 17 percent inflation. Not so good, either.

"So, I decided to begin a new career, and ever since I've been trying to build a business."

That private equity business and the skill, determination, and resourcefulness it took to build it rendered David not only a terrific Lincoln Center trustee but a superb chair of our capital campaign.

As a substantial customer or potential customer of virtually every money-center bank and investment house, David opened doors with ease and allowed Frank Bennack and me to join him in advocating on behalf of Lincoln Center's.

With a sense of humor and of perspective, David advanced Lincoln Center's case as a premier tourist attraction, as a catalytic source of economic development, and as a major contributor to the quality of life in New York City. Indeed, as the only trustee of both Lincoln Center and the Kennedy Center in Washington, D.C., he was in a perfect position to press the case for the physical redevelopment of the nation's first and still the largest and most consequential performing arts center in the world.

I know of no institution anywhere better treated philanthropically by the investment community of New York than Lincoln Center. In no small measure, David is responsible for that accomplishment even as he logged hundreds of thousands of miles each year raising money for another (slightly less) worthy cause—the Carlyle Group. His track record in attracting investors to it also left little to be desired.

John Whitehead

Never was the statement that "most people buy not because they believe, but because the salesman believes" truer than in the case of a philanthropic salesman named John Whitehead.

It was my privilege to serve as the president of the International Rescue Committee when John was its chair. A true believer in the refugee cause, John has been a trustee of the IRC since the Hungarian Revolution in 1956. During that conflict, for a quarter of a century before, and ever since, the IRC has resettled refugees in cities across America and assisted them abroad when uprooted by war, by civil strife, or by the chaos and instability of so many failed states across the Third World.

For John, the refugee cause—bringing the displaced from harm to home—could not be more noble. It offers help to those with the courage to seek a new life for themselves and their families. It aids those fleeing tyranny and in search of freedom. It comes to the side of highly motivated, hardworking people who need only a helping hand to adjust themselves to new living conditions after being uprooted, often suddenly and brutally.

To hear John describe in his own words why, above all others, the needs of refugees and displaced people appealed to him most was to be convinced. The former copresident of Goldman Sachs who transformed that firm's approach to selling had lost none of his advocacy skills several decades after retiring from that distinguished investment firm. Instead, that skill was leavened by a sense of humor and by subsequent experience in government as deputy secretary of state to George Schultz in the Reagan administration and by having served on so many nonprofit boards and government groups, including the Federal Reserve Board, the United Nations Association, the Trilateral Commission, the Boy Scouts of America, the Harvard Business School, and Rockefeller University, among them.

In truth, though, one always had the feeling after joining John on a funding call to, say, David Rockefeller, Jr., or Jerry Speyer, or Arthur Ross, or Rita Hauser, or Josh Weston, that the man articulating the case mattered almost as much as the cause itself.

Having spent a lifetime dispensing advice to others, advocating their careers or *their* civic and charitable interests, how could anyone deny John a meeting, and having met, how could they say no to him? John's fundraising prospects were defenseless in the face of his easygoing, persuasive power. He brought unparalleled authority to his requests because they were the product of a lifetime of devotion to institutions and causes that mattered and because of his own generosity and commitment to them. That track record had so won the respect, affection, and admiration of his colleagues in the business world and his social companions that as often as not I felt like the caboose to the Whitehead fundraising engine.

Frank A. Bennack, Jr.

Frank A. Bennack, Jr., is now the chair of Lincoln Center. A lifelong employee of the Hearst Corporation, Frank spent some 30 years at its headquarters in New York City, 23 as its president and chief executive officer. To hear him, at the age of 75, describe why he decided to complement a busy life as Hearst's vice chair and chair of its Executive Committee, as a member of the board of directors of Wyeth and Polo Ralph Lauren, and as an active trustee of New York-Presbyterian Hospital and the Paley Center for Media, with service as the chair of Lincoln Center is to be riveted. Simply put, Frank allows as how no civic cause post-9/11 could do more to strengthen New York City than to prepare the oldest American and the largest and most consequential performing arts center in the world for the next generation of artists, audiences, and tourists.

Depending on the prospect, Frank would place an accent on the artistic, or the civic, or the tourist, or the economic development dimension of our capital campaign. Always, a meeting began with questions for the prospect about his or her business, family, civic interests, political views, and the like. No one I have ever met listens as well as Frank. No one has a better aptitude for reading nonverbal reactions of prospects or is possessed of better peripheral vision. And no one remembers more clearly an interaction or a disposition on the part of a potential benefactor. He is remarkable.

When a formal presentation concluded, Frank was utterly fearless. He would cite his own financial commitment, that of the Hearst Foundation, those of the prospect's colleagues, associates, or friends, and then he would ask—unflinchingly, without a moment's hesitation—for a specific sum paid out over a period of years.

The self-confidence with which Frank approached a solicitation, combined with his superb preparation about our campaign and about our prospect, made for dazzlingly effective funding calls.

The challenge for me was to get Frank and his trustee colleagues in front of potential donors as early and as often as possible. The track record of results was superb. Frank is a formidable figure, not an easy man to turn down or turn away.

And he, like John Whitehead, had made many more deposits than withdrawals into life's ATM machine of social, civic, and cultural commitment. That healthy bank balance put Frank on the side of the angels when it was he doing the asking rather than what he and his organization found themselves doing most often: giving generously, gracefully, and willingly.

Turnabout is fair play. Comity and reciprocity are reasonable expectations. Disappointments there were, of course. But thanks to Frank and his colleagues, to a terrific cause, to the coalition of city, state, and federal support we had garnered, to the full financial support of our own large board of directors, and to the fact that this campus-wide capital campaign was the first of its kind in Lincoln Center history, setbacks were few and far between.

DONATIONS THAT CAN COST TOO MUCH

Donors can lose their moorings. They can forget what originally drew them to institutions or causes outside themselves. They can overreach by attempting to use their funds to influence the content of a program, the curriculum of a university, the visual artists selected for exhibitions or acquisitions, or, in the case of Lincoln Center, whom we choose to present on the stages of Alice Tully, Avery Fisher, or Rose halls. And the nobility and the selflessness of most charitable acts are undermined by the occasional social climber, publicity seeker, and vain cynosure. How do you decide when a real or potential donor is overreaching and how do you deal with unbecoming conduct?

Deciding where to draw the line pivots off the mission of an institution.

When a distinguished museum like the Guggenheim permits itself to present an exhibit of Armani clothing or of motorcycles, one can be forgiven for believing that crass commercialism has overtaken sound curatorial judgment.

When the Brooklyn Museum features work owned by the exhibit sponsor, as in the case of Charles Saatchi in 1999, or of memorabilia from the film *Star Wars* in 2002, it is fair to ask who is the real donor and who is the real beneficiary.

When New York City's wealthiest private schools seek an agreement with the nonprofit Randall's Island Sports Foundation to be granted exclusive use of public ball fields for their students on weekday afternoons over the next two decades in exchange for a $2.6 million annual "contribution," to help maintain the space, something is deeply wrong. For the children of the public schools of East Harlem and the South Bronx, who would be denied access. For fundamental notions of transparency (the deal was struck behind closed doors) and of governance (no one from East Harlem or the South Bronx, the closest neighborhoods to Randall's Island, serves on the board of directors of the Sports Foundation). Even for the children in the favored private schools who are being taught that if you have enough money and your parents enough clout, you can buy anything, you can even privatize public parks, and you can do so with impunity.[3]

However, when Yale University will not cut the cloth of its undergraduate curriculum or hire faculty members to suit the preferences of a would-be $20 million donor, Lee Bass,[4] or when the Smithsonian tells Catherine Reynolds[5], a patron, that her generosity cannot buy undue influence on exhibit content, a strong message about institutional standards has also been sent. Such a message echoes and reverberates throughout the corridors of the Third Sector.

The same is true when Doctors Without Borders declines financial support from corporations whose activities are judged to conflict with its mission and principles. Illustratively, it will not accept funds from firms doing business with the government of Sudan and therefore indirectly finance genocide in Darfur or benefit from the philanthropy of drug companies that keep the prices of critical medicines too high for the poorest and neediest residents of the Third World. Indeed, since the early 1990s, Doctors Without Borders has not solicited or accepted funds from any companies that derive income from alcohol, tobacco, weapons, pharmaceuticals, medical equipment, biotechnology, oil, mineral, gas, and other extractive industries, such as diamond mining.[6]

For the taste of many, the policy of Doctors Without Borders is perhaps too extreme. Treating whole corporate sectors as if every firm operating in them conducts itself poorly, as if none can demonstrate positive action toward progressive social change, may well paint with too broad a brush. The refusal of some private foundations to invest their assets in the common stock of wide swaths of corporate America is culpable on similar grounds.

Donors deserve perquisites. Parking privileges. Appropriate recognition on a donor wall, on a well-situated plaque, on a building, or at a luncheon or dinner. Even VIP treatment in access to a fine surgeon, or a hospital room with river views, seems reasonable. And individual and institutional donors will adopt policies and take actions with which we may disagree. That is their privilege. After all, every difference of opinion does not rise to the level of a difference in principle.

Looking a gift horse in the mouth too self-righteously, too indiscriminately, could be a self-defeating path to philanthropic penury and to viewing certain institutions and individual donors as permanent adversaries rather than potential partners.

But when the donor endeavors to influence or distort the content of an institution's mission, or compliance with his or her wishes runs the risk of compromising the integrity of academic or artistic or medical judgment, or when its corporate activities run directly counter to its philanthropic offers, then a firm but courteous no thank you is in order.

Put another way, some donors hope for an "insider's advantage," for privileged access. To the degree that these requests can be honored without violating the institution's mission or its ethical standing, that is fine. But if donors overreach, treating the institution as if its purpose were to serve them, not others, then the gift at stake should be politely turned aside. Some donations come at too high a price.

CHAPTER 7

A PASSPORT TO SUCCESSFUL FUNDRAISING: LESSONS OF A LIFETIME

In the first place, I advise you to apply to all those you know who will give you something, next to those whom you are uncertain whether they will give you anything or not and show them the list of those who have given and lastly, do not neglect those whom you are sure will give you nothing, for in some of them, you will be mistaken.

—Benjamin Franklin

He who persuades others to give alms and moves them to act thus, his reward is greater that the reward of him who gives alms himself.

—Maimonides

Woven throughout *Yours for the Asking* are the critical fundraising lessons I have learned as a CEO supplicant, as a trustee solicitor, as a prospective personal donor, as a private foundation trustee, and as the architect and president of the AT&T Foundation.

Here I reduce that guidance to 28 lessons for successful fundraising. Read them carefully. Execute them sharply. Conduct yourself accordingly.

Follow this advice and your track record will markedly improve. That is my pledge. Please redeem it, starting today. In raising money for a worthy cause, there is no time like the present. Hustle is an admired trait among fundraising prospects.

1. DIVERSIFY FUNDING SOURCES

In crafting a fundraising program for your organization or cause, aim to develop a diversified portfolio of supporters: institutional, trustee, individual and governmental. The best protection against downturns in the economy, setbacks in the stock market, or depressed earnings in corporate America is to develop and maintain a judicious mix of stalwart benefactors.

2. DIVERSIFY FUNDING METHODS

Just as the sources of support should be many and varied, so should the methods for raising funds. Ideally, foundation and corporate grant making, business sponsorship, direct mail, special events, major gifts, membership programs, and bequests will all be incorporated into a coherent strategy with each of the component parts supporting one another.

3. IT'S THE BOARD OF DIRECTORS, STUPID

The fundraising equivalent of cultivating your own garden is tending to the growth and flourishing of board giving. It is the foundation on which a sound contributed income program must rest. If trustees are well selected, deeply involved, and highly motivated, then giving generously and getting assiduously becomes habit forming, part of the institutional culture.

4. ADVICE AND MONEY: THE RELATIONSHIP

If what you want is advice, ask for money. If what you want is money, ask for advice. The best fundraisers do not choose between such alternatives.

5. FUNDRAISING: ANYTIME, ANYWHERE, ANY SEASON

There is never a bad season of the year, time of day, or economic climate in which to raise funds for a worthy cause, provided you follow this ironclad rule:

Arrange for an already committed social or professional peer to ask unhesitatingly for a specific sum from a well-qualified prospect who respects the solicitor.

6. THE SOLICITOR'S MAGIC WORDS

There are only three important words for fundraisers to use. There are infinite ways to express them:

Please. (And) thank you.

7. THE RIGHT WAY TO ASK

The most-cited reason for why donors do not give is that they are not asked.

Or they are not asked by the right peer solicitor who has already given generously to the cause or organization.

Or the case for donating is too complex and not sufficiently compelling.

So ask early. Ask often. Ask persuasively. State your case simply and succinctly.

Most of all, convince the right donor who enjoys a strong relationship to the prospect to ask with you.

Remember, donors give to people they admire, not just causes and organizations they respect.

8. SHOE LEATHER TRUMPS MAIL

It is harder to turn down a request to meet face to face for 50 minutes than a written proposal for $50,000. Meetings are more important than mail. In fundraising, shoe leather trumps the keyboard or the telephone almost always.

9. NO IS NOT AN ANSWER

For great fundraisers, no is just the beginning of a conversation.

In the face of resistance or rejection, stay poised, remain resilient, and do not lose that sense of perspective or humor.

10. BASEBALL, NOT A COLLEGE EXAM

Remember, fundraising is not a college test. In a college exam, if you answer one out of every two or three questions correctly, it is more than likely you have flunked.

Fundraising is more akin to baseball. In baseball, one hit for every three times at bat secures a .333 batting average. Those who enjoy such season averages are most valuable players.

As an MVP, your team hopes you will step up to bat (solicit) more often.

11. FUNDRAISING AS APPLE PIE

Everyone you meet or converse with is a potential donor. Giving is an act of citizenship. It is red, white, and blue. It is patriotic. It is motherhood and apple pie. It is quintessentially American. If donations and money are to nonprofit organizations what voting is to democracy, it is worth observing that more than twice as many Americans participate in the Third Sector as cast a ballot in presidential elections.

Requesting a gift is a favor to the potential donor. It is an act of flattery. It offers the opportunity to move beyond worldly success to social consequence. It provides another path to self-realization. Responding favorably insures a better night's sleep.

Why would you wish to deprive anyone of such benefits and opportunities?

12. FUNDRAISING IS A TEAM EFFORT

Build a staff possessed of energy, curiosity, resilience, and humor. Build a staff that communicates well, orally and in writing. Build a staff that reads widely, mixes and mingles easily, and listens well.

13. PRACTICE, PRACTICE

In fundraising, an ounce of experience is worth a pound of logic.

Successful fundraisers become that way just as students graduate from the Juilliard School: They practice, practice, practice.

14. PHILANTHROPY IS BIOGRAPHY

Philanthropy is biography. Take the time to learn your prospective donor's background, interests, professional history, and family composition. Getting to yes is often more than just a matter of analysis and manifest need. It is solving the mystery of what really moves your prospect to do something special for a cause. If you appeal to something deeply personal or respond to values sharply felt, the prospect is bound to become the highly valued donor.

15. SPEED AND AGILITY MATTER

In soliciting donors in writing, it is far better to be roughly right, brief, and early, than perfect, comprehensive, and late. Breaking through the clutter of the busy lives of donors and grabbing their attention requires speed as well as merit. The race often goes to the swift, not the fastidious.

16. THE CORPORATE/NONPROFIT MEETING PLACE

To be successful in securing corporate donations or sponsorships, find the intersections between business interest and nonprofit need. Locate them and you will unlock the safe containing not only what remains of corporate philanthropy but of marketing, advertising, sales, sponsorship, and employee relations resources.

17. THE SCHOOL OF HARD KNOCKS

Fundraising is a learning process. In a first-class development operation, mistakes occur every day, and strikeouts are inevitable. Critical to improvement are structured opportunities to diagnose error, to engage in postmortems, to improve over time. Doing so also requires two qualities: an eagerness to learn and a very thick skin.

18. EARLY MONEY: THE BEST KIND

When raising funds to launch a new initiative, to start a novel program, to begin a fresh fiscal year, or to initiate a capital campaign, remember EMILY. EMILY is the acronym for a political action organization. It stands for "early money is like yeast." EMILY should be the rallying cry to guide your development efforts.

Fundraising is a deeply psychological, confidence-building process. No one wishes to fund a cause or institution that appears to be lost or failing. No one wants to feel alone in responding to an appeal. Your strategy should always be to start soon, to pick low-hanging fruit—friends of the organization who can be relied on to support it—and then to enlarge that base going forward.

It is not for nothing that our American sage Benjamin Franklin observed, "To give early is to give twice."

19. DONORS CRAVE RECOGNITION

No matter what they tell you, most donors yearn for recognition and identity. The great philosopher Maimonides argued that giving anonymously was a higher form of charity. After all, the intention should be to advance a cause, not oneself. But Maimonides knew not of donors as a class of philanthropists who hardly mind the celebrity, the social status, the business connections, or the prestige associated with a well-publicized gift. Rare is the donor interested only in doing good. Figuring out how best to acknowledge benefactors is no small challenge for able fundraisers.

20. PHILANTHROPISTS NEED HELP

Wealthy people and grant-making institutions need assistance. More often than they will ever admit, it is very difficult to know what to do with "surplus capital." Julius Rosenwald, a major leader of Sears, Roebuck and a distinguished philanthropist, put the matter candidly and well: "It is nearly always easier to earn one million dollars honestly than to dispose of it wisely."

Great fundraisers help donors. Fundraisers specialize in dispensing the "wisdom" that Rosenwald finds so scarce. They often do so in writing, as in the preparation of well-tailored proposals.

21. MERIT MATTERS

Merit attracts interest and money. In fundraising, there is nothing better than a good idea to capture the imagination and facilitate a successful solicitation. Donors love to help bridge the gap between an institution's promise and its performance. Do not fail to give them that opportunity. Remember, you are not pleading for support. You are dispensing favors to the fortunate.

22. REPUTATION: HARD TO ACQUIRE, EASY TO SQUANDER

At bottom, most adults are insecure about themselves and their points of view. They look for validation, even in their philanthropic choices. A friend of mine puts it this way: Nothing is real unless it's virtual. And in New York City at least, if your institution or cause receives prominent and favorable coverage in the *New York Times*, the virtual becomes real. Translation: Positive and generous media relations is a terrific fundraising asset. It says to the donor, "You are joining forces with a winner." Marshall McLuhan's phrase, "The medium is the message," carries an important lesson for fundraisers.

23. COMMUNICATE, EARLY AND OFTEN

Consider the donor and the prospect valued members of your extended team. Communicate with them about your progress, early and often. Asking for financial support should be a natural extension of a relationship, not a sudden "surprise." Repairing to a donor or a prospect only when you need help is a surefire route to a firm declination.

24. ROLES THAT FUNDRAISERS PLAY

Fundraisers see the world differently from normal folk. They read the social pages to ferret out who is looking for favorable attention and on behalf of what causes. They study the business section of the newspaper to learn whose fortunes are swelling and whose are declining. They watch for which parts of the economy are faring well even in down markets. They know the locations that are the most desirable in which to live, the restaurants that are hot, and the in places to vacation. The first-class fundraiser is part sociologist, part psychologist, and part investigative reporter. The first-class fundraiser is also a terrific conversationalist. And the raw material for those conversations can be found in the right newspapers, periodicals, and books, on the right Web sites, and at the right parties.

Fundraisers need to balance carefully research behind a desk and getting out of the office to meet prospects. The money is out there, not in here. Insularity and complacency are a fundraiser's curse.

25. PLAN AND PREPARE

Your chances for success with a potential donor will vary in direct proportion to the distance in time between your request and when it needs to be honored.

If you wish someone to chair a gala or other fundraising event, ask at least a year in advance. You are far more likely to receive a yes when seeking a donor's leadership role or a charitable gift if the request does not appear driven by an immediate, pressing need or by lack of preparation.

Be flexible. About the size of the gift. About the timing. And about terms of payment.

Be grateful for whatever the response.

Building and sustaining long-term friends for your institution or cause is the objective.

Always leave room (to ask) for more later (and for help in rallying others to your side).

The essence of first-rate fundraising is sound planning, excellent preparation, and superb execution.

Much as in sports, a good game plan is a critical success factor in fundraising. The baseball player's swing of a bat, the tennis player's racquet forehand, and the football quarterback's pass all need to anticipate the next move. A skeet shooter aims the rifle not for where the target is but for where it will be.

You and your staff must think ahead—to the next ask, the follow-on special event, the to-be-developed proposal. Building such forward-looking discipline into your daily work is the sign of a first-class operation.

26. SPREAD THE GOSPEL

Once you have secured an important donor, ask for help. What friends, colleagues, or peers in the same field (foundation, corporation, small business) might also be attracted to supporting your cause? Your best advocates are your existing donors. Do not hesitate to request their assistance. Be specific. And be thankful. The most important transition in philanthropy has to do with pronouns. When "your" cause or campaign becomes "our" cause or campaign, you have won not just a supporter but an ally, a comrade in "alms."

In politics, the effort to enlist a donor's help has become institution-alized. Those who not only give but get are referred to as aggregators or bundlers. For tapping their social and business connections by mail, by telephone, and by special event, these political campaign solicitors are highly regarded and very well treated by campaigns, candidates, and office holders seeking reelection.

Fundraisers for charitable institutions would do well to emulate the methods by which successful political fundraisers enlist their supporters to give and to get "until it hurts."

27. FUNDRAISING IS ALL ABOUT TOMORROW

Prepare your institution for its fundraising future. Do not neglect culti-vating bequests. Invest in soliciting the gifts and participation of young people. Enlarge your board of trustees and raise its members' sights for giving and getting. Pay attention to new and enhanced sources of wealth by occupation (e.g., hedge funds and private equity managers, commercial real estate developers), by area of the country (e.g., Silicon Valley, New York City, Houston, Dallas), and of the world (e.g., the Middle East, BRIC [Brazil, Russia, India, and China], and northern Europe, including Britain and Scandinavia), and by company as a collec-tivity of wealthy executives rather than just as a firm (e.g., Microsoft, Google, Amazon, Apple, Exxon, Oracle).

28. LEAVING A LEGACY

Leave not only a board but a staff much stronger than you found it. Set high performance expectations. Insist that they be satisfied. When hir-ing employees, select, don't settle. And don't hesitate to ask underper-formers to leave. Overcome your reluctance to "fire." More often than not, dismissal with dignity and a path to the next post will come as a relief to the recipient of bad news. The magic, nonjudgmental message that almost always fits the bill goes as follows: "George, this just isn't working, is it? Let us help find a better place for your talents to be applied to best advantage."

Hires who do not work out are often as much the fault of the employer as the employee. Acknowledge that reality. Learn from it. The successor you select (don't settle) is bound to be better.

CHAPTER 8

HUMOR AND
FUNDRAISING

He who gives
While he lives
Also knows
Where it goes

—Eli Broad, quoting an anonymous source

Apart from energy and resilience, perhaps nothing is needed more in a fundraiser than a sense of humor. And maybe that is why there are so many terrific jokes about separating people from a small portion of their material wealth for the benefit of others.

Humor relaxes the prospect. It lessens, if not removes entirely, the seriousness and awkwardness of a solicitation. It softens the occasion. Humor puts the request into the proper perspective. After all, no negative answer has ever caused the sky to fall. And humor renders the whole process more fun for both the volunteers and the professionals.

A sense of levity also helps to keep your volunteer solicitor colleagues highly motivated. Their lives are extremely busy. If working on your institution's behalf and at your side is viewed as more pleasurable than burdensome, more enjoyable than heavy lifting, that is all to the good.

What follows are some of the best jokes, quips, and witticisms that I have heard over the years. They have worked for me in one-on-one meetings, in speeches, and as a social lubricant for fellow solicitors and prospects.

Try them on for size.

Included among them are some sayings from Frank Bennack, who chaired Lincoln Center during most of our massive redevelopment construction and fundraising project. I'm partial to him. He's my boss. Elsewhere, I have described how Frank is an excellent fundraiser. Humor is yet another reason for that well-deserved status as solicitor extraordinaire.

Smart and courtly, well prepared and an excellent listener, upbeat and highly motivated, Frank also brought to the solicitation process a zest for identifying the light side of an interaction or a mood. No chapter on humor and fundraising would be complete without reference to some of his lore.

THE RELENTLESSNESS OF FUNDRAISERS

Two IBM executives are flying in a private jet to an appointment overseas. The pilot encounters air turbulence and is forced to crash land on a very remote and very beautiful island.

The jet is immobilized and the pilot loses his life. But miraculously, the two IBM executives emerge unscathed.

One immediately observes the remoteness of the island and concludes that rescue is highly unlikely. He forages for wood, begins building a shelter, and gathers food for what will likely be a very long stay.

The second executive takes a completely different approach. He goes for a swim. He jogs along the beach. He assembles a makeshift sun reflector and listens to his favorite CD.

Finally, in frustration, the industrious IBMer says to his laidback colleague, "Why do you diagnose our situation so differently from me?"

He replies, "It's simple. I've only been at IBM for one year. But in that year I pledged $10,000 to the United Way, $5,000 to Catholic Charities of New York, and $1,000 to Lincoln Center. I've not made a single payment on any of these pledges.

"Don't worry. They'll find us. They'll find us."

THE ELUSIVENESS OF PROSPECTS

The priest stands in the middle of a crumbling church on a rainy day sermonizing right beneath a badly leaking roof.

In frustration, he turns to the congregation and says, "For the past six months I have been appealing to you for donations to help repair this church and I regret to report that virtually nothing has been volunteered, so with apologies I must ask Mr. O'Malley to please stand up.

"Mr. O'Malley, everyone knows that you are by far the wealthiest member of this church. Why can't you set a positive example?"

O'Malley replies, "Father, you may not know this, but my wife is bedridden, severely incapacitated, and requires 24-hour nursing care. My son is enrolled in medical school, and tuition, room, and board are very costly. And my daughter, God bless her, is an undergraduate at Duke University. Coping with her expenses could be staggering.

"However, I don't help any of them.

Why should I help you?"

FUNDRAISING IS HEAVY LIFTING

The penultimate act in the latest Barnum & Bailey Circus is the Strong Man. With the spotlight on him and with drums rolling, he holds up before the crowd in Madison Square Garden a relatively small grapefruit. Immediately in front of him is a table on which sit two extremely large pitchers.

At the count of three, he takes the grapefruit in his left hand and begins squeezing it. Amazingly, juice emerges from the grapefruit far beyond what anyone might think it could possibly hold. The first pitcher totally overflows with grapefruit juice.

Remaining in the hand of the weight lifter is a dried-up rind. He looks out before 18,000 people and says, "If there is anyone in the audience who can get a single drop out of the remaining grapefruit to fall into the second pitcher, you and your family are entitled to attend the circus anywhere in the world, free of charge, all expenses paid."

An old man, about 80 years old, is the only one to raise his hand and comes sauntering down the aisle. He takes the rind from the weight lifter and starts squeezing. Not only does the man squeeze out a few drops, he manages to fill the entire second pitcher.

The audience and weightlifter are stunned.

"What's your name, sir?" asked the Strong Man.

"Irving Shapiro," replies the old man.

"What did you do for a living, Mr. Shapiro?"

The old man shrugs. "I was a fundraiser for the UJA."

THE IMPERATIVE OF DONOR RECOGNITION

In his advancing years, Henry Ford decided to visit his ancestral home in Ireland.

As you can imagine, the villagers were extremely excited by the prospect of one of the richest men in the world returning to his roots.

When he landed in Dublin Airport, a group of townspeople were at the gate to greet his arrival. They followed him on the road for the 90-minute trip to the place Henry Ford called home.

On arrival, they gathered at what passed for a town hall, and one of the villagers, in a moment of great excitement, departed from the carefully scripted arrangement by blurting out the following lines:

"Mr. Ford, I'm sure you know that we are about to build a community hospital here in the village. We would appreciate a generous contribution from you."

Ford, somewhat thunderstruck by the immediacy of the request, said, "Okay. I'd be pleased to contribute $5,000."

He bid the villagers good night and looked forward to seeing them in the morning for breakfast.

The next morning, the solicitor of the funds came running into the dining room white as a sheet. "Mr. Ford," he said, "I'm terribly sorry to report that there is a most egregious mistake in this morning's newspaper. What's worse, sir, the error involves you. Still worse, sir, it is in the headline on the front page." Whereupon he unfurled the newspaper whose headline read in bold, large letters: "HENRY FORD LAUNCHES VILLAGE HOSPITAL CAMPAIGN WITH UNPRECE-DENTED GIFT OF $50,000."

The flustered villagers watched the stunned Henry Ford read the headline. The spokesperson solicitor was quick to say "Don't worry, Mr. Ford. We intend to print a retraction in bold, equally large print in tomorrow's newspaper!"

Ford, having regained his composure, allowed as how that was not necessary. Instead, he would stand behind the $50,000 pledge. Or, to be more accurate, the $45,000 "mistake."

However, Ford said he needed the villagers to keep a pledge of their own. When the hospital opened, the plaque that was unveiled needed to be prepared by Mr. Ford and not seen by anyone until it was revealed officially in opening ceremonies.

Five years later that day came to pass.

The plaque was uncovered and it read:

> I came unto you as a stranger and you took me in.
>
> —Matthew

THE LORE OF FRANK BENNACK, JR.

He is so stingy he throws quarters at you like they were manhole covers!

That guy is stingy? How stingy? Well, let me put it this way: I've never met *anyone* with deeper pockets and shorter arms!

Beverly Sills was a world-class fundraiser. Charismatic. Magnetic. Incorrigible. Persuasive. Why, she could charm a dog right off a meat wagon.

You've thrown your hat over the fence. Now go fetch it.

He's all hat and no cattle.

So it has come to this. Everyone now says when Frank Bennack gets you on the phone, it is always a collect call.

POLITICS IS INEXPENSIVE

The kind of fundraising I do is never less than $25,000 a solicitation. Most often more.

The upper limit on funds one can give to a presidential candidate is $4,300 in total for both the primary and the general election.

Which is why I would probably be a terrific political fundraiser.

If I call, write, or drop by asking for *only* $4,300, most folks would breathe with a sigh of relief and respond favorably, instantaneously.

MAJOR PROSPECTS ENJOY HEALTHY EGOS

He's a self-made man who admires his creator.

He's a legend in his own mind.

SELF-DEPRECATING HUMOR: IT WEARS WELL

Pete Peterson is a legendary figure in investment and domestic and foreign policy circles. He was secretary of commerce in the Nixon administration, chairman and CEO of Lehman Brothers, a cofounder of the Blackstone Group, a leading private equity firm, a longtime chair of the Council on Foreign Relations and of the Institute for International Economics (now the Peterson Institute), and for purposes of this story, most importantly, the founder of the Concord Coalition, a group devoted to balanced budgets and to coping with long-term economic challenges, such as the financing of Social Security and Medicare.

One of Pete's best friends is Ted Sorensen, the former chief speechwriter and special assistant to President Kennedy and a longtime senior partner of Paul, Weiss, Rifkind, Wharton & Garrison, a leading international law firm based in New York City.

As Pete tells it, both he and Ted are in a jet plane when it is hijacked. The perpetrators assure the passengers that they are only interested in killing Peterson and Sorensen, so everyone else should remain calm.

Both are granted a last wish.

Peterson asks for ten minutes to use the PA system to warn all passengers about the danger of unfunded liabilities in our pension system, our growing inability to finance Medicare and Social Security, and the challenges posed by the aging of the workforce in America and in Western Europe.

Sorensen allows as how if they grant Peterson that last request, then his own wish is to be killed first, right away, before Pete gets started.

A CLASSIC: MANY VARIATIONS ON A THEME

The four egregious lies:

1. The check is in the mail.

2. What I'm about to do won't hurt you a bit.

3. Of course I'll respect you in the morning.

4. I'm from a foundation (corporation, branch of government), and I'm here to help you.

SHE WAS ONE OF A KIND: BEVERLY SILLS—PART A

"The Cold Call"

Beverly Sills was not only an impressive fundraiser, she was also a willing solicitor. At 73 years of age, during the last six months of her eight-year term as the chair of Lincoln Center, I witnessed her place a cold call to a prospect. It went something like this:

"Mr. Zilinsky, good morning. My name is Beverly Sills. I'm 73 years of age. I understand that you are 69. And mutual friends of ours can hardly believe that we have never met."

"Name two," says Zilinsky.

"They've suggested that I call you so we can get together soon."

"Name two," says Zilinsky.

Beverly, ignoring Zilinsky's apparent toughness, just plows ahead.

"So look at your calendar for next week. Would you prefer breakfast on Tuesday or lunch on Wednesday? Just name the time and place and I'll be there."

"Well, okay, how about Wednesday, 12:30 P.M. at the Four Seasons."

"Good. See you then."

On Wednesday at 3:00 P.M. Beverly returned to the office. She allowed as how she had paid for lunch, but Mr. Zilinsky, whom she rather liked, had paid for next summer's Mostly Mozart Festival.

SHE WAS ONE OF A KIND: BEVERLY SILLS—PART B

"Fundraising as Striptease"

I vividly recall a visit from Beverly Sills, the world-famous diva who at the time was general director of the New York City Opera. She came to call on me in my capacity as the president of the AT&T Foundation. What occasioned the meeting was truly an emergency. All of the opera company's costumes had been destroyed the week before in a New Jersey warehouse fire.

With characteristic poise and conviction, Sills asked for an immediate grant to help restore a costume collection for the opera company.

I asked her whether she had approached any other firm and wondered why AT&T was on her calling card since while the company had been generous to many Lincoln Center constituents, it had not given a grant to the New York City Opera.

She replied, "Dear Reynold. The alphabet. I start at the beginning."

Possessed not only of persuasive skills, Sills also enjoyed a boisterous sense of humor. Allowing as how the need was urgent and compelling, she made it abundantly clear that leaving my office without a pledge of at least $100,000 was quite out of the question.

And when I hesitated, she asked whether, since her dancers, singers, and chorus members were without costumes, would it help if she disrobed then and there?

I declined that offer. Beverly left with a $100,000 pledge.

SHE WAS ONE OF A KIND: BEVERLY SILLS—PART C

"Change the Name: Double the Gift"

Soon after Beverly became the general director of the New York City Opera, she hailed a cab to take her across town to see her old friend Douglas Dillon, the former secretary of the treasury under President Kennedy, founder of the white-shoe investment firm Dillon Read, and then the chair of the Metropolitan Museum of Art.

After an initial exchange of warm greetings, Beverly launched into a description of the plight of the New York City Opera as a prelude to asking for a donation.

Dillon said, in effect, Bev, relax, I know why you are here. No need to elaborate. Let's gossip for a while.

After about 15 minutes of pleasant exchange filled with laughter, Dillon summoned his secretary and asked for his checkbook.

She returned with a huge, leather-bound check binder. He reached for his quill fountain pen, dipped it in an inkwell, wrote out a check, and folded it carefully. He placed it in a sealed envelope and handed it to Beverly as a sign of his respect and affection for her and the institution she led.

Beverly hailed a cab on Fifth Avenue for the trip back to Lincoln Center. Having just retired as the world's leading soprano and unaccustomed to fundraising, Beverly couldn't wait to open the envelope.

And when she did, there was a check for a disappointing $50,000, made out not to the New York City Opera but to the Metropolitan Opera!

Beverly's first act in returning to her office was to pick up the phone and call Douglas Dillon.

"Douglas," she said, "thank you for your check. I'm returning it to you for two reasons. First, you made it out to the wrong opera company. And second, the figure is missing a zero."

A week later $500,000 was deposited into the account of the New York City Opera.

AN EXCUSABLE LATENESS

I served for over a decade as a trustee of one of America's leading non-profit theaters, the Manhattan Theater Club.

For four of those years I chaired its Development Committee and in that capacity solicited gifts, principally from companies, as I was then myself a senior officer at AT&T.

One wintry morning I arrived at Banker's Trust on a funding call to its president. I was to meet the board chair, Michael Coles, a retired investment banker at Goldman Sachs who loved MTC and who was generous to it in all conceivable ways.

In the president's anteroom I found not Michael but the terrific team of Lynne Meadow and Barry Grove, respectively the artistic director and managing director of MTC.

As it was 8:05 A.M., and our appointment was for 8:00 and Michael was always punctual, I asked Lynne and Barry why they were present and about Michael's whereabouts.

"Michael called us very early this morning and asked us to meet you in his stead. He profusely apologizes, but his plane wouldn't start today!"

Ever since retiring, Michael tried to spend most of his time out in the Hamptons at his home on Shelter Island. To render his commute to Manhattan easier, he would regularly fly his own plane to the White Plains airport and be picked up by a limousine and chauffeured to Manhattan.

On this morning it was not to be.

And ever since, on the very rare occasion when I am ever late on a fundraising call (a no-no, if ever there is one when soliciting charitable gifts), I utter to myself, if not out loud, "I'm sorry not to be here on time, but my plane wouldn't start."

INTRODUCING A GALA HONOREE

The words of Alan Batkin, of the board of directors of the International Rescue Committee:

Last year the International Rescue Committee honored one of its own, Andy Grove, known to the world as the founder and CEO of Intel but known to the IRC as a refugee. Fleeing Budapest, he crawled 20 miles across the Hungarian border in 1956 with $20 in his pocket to freedom in Vienna.

Tonight we honor Michael Bloomberg, a refugee from Salomon Brothers who fled uptown in a limousine with a severance check for $10 million.

THE ASK REDUCED TO ITS ESSENTIALS

I vividly recall accompanying John Whitehead on a fundraising call to Arthur Ross, his friend of many decades.

Arthur was a noted philanthropist in New York City. While modest and unassuming in person, he did enjoy leaving his name attached to many of his charitable gifts. And why not?

As a result, you can visit the Arthur Ross Pinetum in Central Park, the Arthur Ross Green House at Barnard College, the Ross Terrace and Garden at the Cooper-Hewitt National Design Museum, the Arthur Ross Book Award Ceremony at the Council on Foreign Relations, the Arthur Ross Garden at Mt. Sinai Medical Center, the Arthur and Janet Ross Lecture Hall at the New York Botanical Garden, and many more.

Arthur was John's guest at the Links Club, a prestigious watering hole for corporate officialdom, investment bankers, and distinguished lawyers, among others. They talked about Arthur's place in Jamaica and about his golf game. As fellow trustees, they compared notes about the state of the United Nations Association. They bemoaned the condition of the Links Club white wine list, which featured Chardonnay, with nary a decent Sauvignon Blanc to be found. For John and Arthur, most Chardonnays are to white wine what Welch's grape juice is to red.

Suddenly Arthur turned to me and asked for an explanation of what the International Rescue Committee does and why it needed his assistance.

I told Arthur that the IRC helps refugees in two ways—by providing assistance to them abroad while internally displaced in their own country or after fleeing into a third nation and by resettling them in the United States. He seemed more interested in the second part of its mission and asked me to elaborate.

So I told Arthur that the IRC first validates the status of refugees abroad with the Immigration and Naturalization Service (INS). After proving that they fled in fear of persecution and cannot return without grave risk or that they were entitled to reunite with spouse or sibling in America, they were then transported by air to one of 17 cities around the United States. Upon landing, IRC personnel, often supplemented by volunteers, meet the refugees at the airport, settle them into temporary housing, and begin an intensive three-month orientation—to America, to the city that was their new home, to schools, hospitals, and mass transportation. The IRC helps to secure appropriate identification papers and, if necessary, arranges for classes in English and/or in vocational skills and/or in recredentialing those who were already trained as teachers, nurses, physicians, engineers, and the like in their home country.

No matter what their circumstances, the IRC stressed the need to find employment, temporary though it may be, in the shortest possible time. And I noted that the IRC was very proud of the track record of its clients. Within 90 days, 90 percent of the heads of households of the refugees it settled from around the world—Africa, Asia, the Balkans—were working full time.

"Oh, I see," said Arthur. "No wonder John Whitehead loves this cause. Let me summarize. The IRC takes refugees from the INS to the IRS within three months of arriving in the U.S."

That day I felt doubly blessed—for Arthur's gift of $100,000 (it would have been more, he needled John, if his host had offered a decent white wine!) and for capturing the IRC's resettlement mission as pithily and cogently as I had ever heard it uttered.

I quote Arthur Ross's one-sentence view of refugee resettlement in speech after speech, an attribution that Arthur would have appreciated, although it was not anticipated as a part of his gift. It came without restrictions of any kind.

INTELLECTUAL FLIGHT AND AN EMPTY WALL NO MORE

One fine morning I found myself in Washington, D.C., to, among other things, join David Rubenstein, the founder of the Carlyle Group and a trustee of Lincoln Center who chaired our capital campaign, on a funding call to SBC.

When it concluded, I hopped in David's car for a quick trip to his Washington office. I was struck by its modest size and by the fact that its walls were bare, although a number of pictures and photographs were propped up in corners of David's working space.

I thought that perhaps he had just moved into new quarters. No, I was told, David's office location had not changed in 16 years. His walls were bare because he could not decide what to put where.

Soon after, David was interviewed for *Business Week* by Maria Bartiromo, made famous in business circles for her scintillating and intelligent presence on CNBC, where she was affectionately and admiringly referred to as Money Honey.

After posing a few tough-minded business questions, Maria asked David about whether it was becoming harder or easier to recruit the best and the brightest business school graduates into private equity.

David waxed eloquent. When I was a kid, he allowed, parents wanted their offspring to be a doctor or a lawyer. Not today. Now dads and moms want their children to work in hedge fund or private equity firms. In fact, there is now a veritable flight of intellectual capital to the alternative investment industry.

"Which is why," David concluded, "I have no intention of being operated on in the next decade or so."

In a flash, it occurred to me that I had the makings of a couple of cartoons that David would especially appreciate. I called a brilliant designer colleague, Peter Duffin, and described what I thought would be humorous enough to capture David's fancy. The two cartoon versions we sent to David as framed gifts may be found in Exhibits 8.1 and 8.2.

EXHIBIT **8.1**   *Duffin Version #1*

"David, don't worry. I used to be in private equity."

EXHIBIT **8.2** *Duffin Version #2*

"David, there's no reason to be nervous. I switched to medicine later in life. Spent 20 years in private equity."

Guess what?

David's walls are bare no longer.

THE PHILANTHROPIC MARINE CORPS

Question: What's the best way to find Osama bin Laden?

Answer: Send a million-dollar pledge to the Lincoln Center development office in his name and leave the return address blank.

CHAPTER 9

FUNDRAISING: DIMENSIONS OF THE FUTURE

The defining and ongoing innovations of this age—biotechnology, the computer, the Internet—give us a chance we've never had before to end extreme poverty and death from preventable disease . . .
Members of the Harvard Family: Here in the Yard is one of the great collections of intellectual talent in the world.

What for?

—Bill Gates

The American people are a generous lot. Our country's multiplying challenges are severe. This nation's Third Sector is a vital source of problem-solving energy and a place where civic leadership is welcome.

What stands between so many of our social ills and effective programs to prevent and remedy them are adequate resources.

The nation's army of professional and volunteer solicitors are fully capable of identifying enhanced and new sources of giving and of raising funds in unprecedented sums.

Toward that noble end, it is my hope that *Yours for the Asking* offers useful advice and actionable intelligence.

Raising our expectations for giving and asking, for what it means to be an honored benefactor or a generous trustee, and for what is entailed by intelligent, passionate solicitation matters a great deal to the health of our country.

Elections are critical in our democracy. The role of government at all levels is indispensable to a vital society. Importantly, America needs a healthy economy and the competitive corporations and small businesses that undergird it. They are indispensable to the existence of thriving, generous individual benefactors and philanthropic institutions.

But this country like no other enjoys a rich, vibrant, multifaceted Third Sector. It is at once a realm of domestic life that welcomes social and civic vitality and that generates solutions to some of America's most pressing challenges.

To seize them will require change.

THE BOARD OF DIRECTORS TRANSFORMED

I envision the day when the forces of globalization more dramatically shape the composition of nonprofit boards of directors.

In the twenty-first century, how can it be that such international institutions of worldwide renown like Lincoln Center, the Metropolitan Museum of Art, Stanford University, the Cleveland Clinic, and Johns Hopkins Hospital hardly have any trustees on their boards of directors carrying a foreign passport?

It is passing strange, is it not, that most of the members of the boards of quintessentially global organizations live within walking distance from them.

If the curators of the Metropolitan Museum of Art fluently speak dozens of languages and guide the acquisition of art from painters and sculptors on every continent and from every century, if Lincoln Center's programs attract musicians, singers, directors, and conductors from around the world performing repertory drawn from its four corners, then surely the governance of both institutions, and many others, would benefit from perspectives and financial support born of cosmopolitan experience and temperament.

WILLIE SUTTON GOES GLOBAL

It is said that Willie Sutton robbed banks because there you would find money. Today, these banks are located more and more in Russia, Dubai, Qatar, China, India, and Brazil. Isn't it past time for savvy nonprofits to seek involvement of leading citizens from these countries and from Western Europe?

Although it is true that the American tax system provides generous incentives for charitable gifts largely unknown outside of our borders, nonprofits in many of the countries I have named are not shy about raising money here in America for their Third Sector. Friends of Oxford and Cambridge universities. Friends of the Royal Shakespeare, the National, the Donmar and the Almeida theatres. Friends of the Tate, the Louvre, and the Hermitage. Friends of the Bolshoi Ballet and the White Knight Foundation. Friends of the Israel Museum, the Hebrew University of Jerusalem, and the Israel Philharmonic. Friends of Venice. They all flourish here on our shores.

Isn't turnabout fair play? As foreign companies succeed in America and as entrepreneurs and investors from abroad grow wealthy thanks in no small measure to American firms and consumers, shouldn't we expect them to contribute a small share of their gains to worthy nonprofit institutions and causes?

When in Rome, one should do as the Romans do. But that will not happen, unless we ask.

As the dollar depreciates against most other currencies, as sovereign funds from abroad purchase stakes in our leading companies, money center and investment banks, hedge and private equity funds, the visibility and accessibility of their new owners increases commensurately.

In New York City, more and more of our best and most expensive condominium housing is being purchased by foreigners who visit our museums, attend our performing arts centers, matriculate in our universities, and seek cures for what ails them in our hospitals and medical centers.

Many with the wealth and resources to give some of it away are already in our midst. Bestirring ourselves to find them and convince them of our merits is a new frontier. Those who cross into it will be richly rewarded.

Two important examples will substantiate the case.

First, there has in recent years been a surge of wealth in Britain as its financial center in London vies with New York City to be the largest home for hedge fund managers and private equity investors. In 2006, fully 485,000 individuals in Britain had more than $1 million to invest, apart from their first homes, up 8.1 percent from the year before. In fact, according to Merrill Lynch & Co. and the consulting firm Capgemini, the United Kingdom is now the place where 17 percent of Europe's multimillionaires domicile.

That rising wealth is driving up charitable giving. According to Britain's Charities Aid Foundation, individuals in England gave a total of $18.4 billion in 2006, up 9 percent from 2005.

This generosity flows from several causes, apart from individuals enjoying the wherewithal to voluntarily donate funds.

The affluent in Britain, as in the United States and all around the world, are surrounded by the rapid growth of nonprofit organizations that comprise the Third Sector. Their size, scale, and impact render philanthropy more natural and more sought after. Both nonprofit supply and demand are increasing at a very rapid pace virtually everywhere. A leading scholar of the Third Sector overseas, Lester Salamon of Johns Hopkins University, has characterized their rise as nothing short of revolutionary.

> The scope and scale of this phenomenon [people on every continent forming associations to deliver human services, promote economic development, prevent environmental degradation, protect civil rights . . .] are immense. Indeed, we are in the midst of a global "associational revolution" that may prove as significant to the latter twentieth century as the rise of the nation-state to the nineteenth.[1]

In the United Kingdom, 4 percent of all employees work in the Third Sector and 4.8 percent of its gross domestic product emanates from nonprofits. Although these figures are understated because they exclude all religious-sponsored activity, they are impressive because citizens and corporations in the United Kingdom do not receive nearly as extravagant tax benefits as do their counterparts in America.

Given the combination of quantitative impact and qualitative heft, it is no wonder that the U.K. affluent, like their counterparts all over the world, are doing more than taking notice. They are acting as philanthropists and as volunteers.

What is more, their investors, their customers, and their competitors are increasingly calling attention to nonprofits as problem solvers, as sources of societal energy, as causes of social cohesion, and as accumulators of social capital.

It is no wonder, then, that other nations yearn for the pluralism, the excellence, and the innovation emanating from a mature Third Sector like the one America enjoys.

In perhaps the most dramatic example of this quest for integrating Third Sector principles and practices into new settings, Abu Dhabi, the capital of the United Arab Emirates, agreed to a $1.267 billion package of support to the Louvre Abu Dhabi, a new museum to be built as part of a $27 billion tourist, residential, and cultural development on Saadiyat Island. The French architect for the museum is Pritzker Prize winner Jean Nouvel, and its 260,000-foot complex will be planned from design to construction by him and then operated by the Louvre.

As part of this deal, the French Ministry of Culture will receive $520 million for use of the Louvre name over 30 years. In addition, Abu Dhabi will donate $325 million to the Louvre itself to refurbish a wing. Two other features of the agreement are also breathtaking. The Louvre will be paid $214.2 million over 20 years for its management expertise, and it will provide four temporary exhibits per year for 15 years in exchange for $253.5 million.[2]

This stunning development comes on top of a very lucrative arrangement with the Guggenheim Museum. It will provide similar services in overseeing a Frank Gehry–built Abu Dhabi Guggenheim to be opened by 2012 and, for all intents and purposes, operated by the Guggenheim. Payment for services rendered and a philanthropic gift coming the Guggenheim's way are also measured well in excess of $100 million.[3]

This deal negotiated by Thomas Krens, the Guggenheim's globetrotting director, supplements the Guggenheim Bilbao in northern Spain, its annex in Berlin, and its traditional outpost in Venice, where the Peggy Guggenheim Collection is housed. Similarly, the Pompidou Centre is overseeing the management of a new contemporary art museum in Shanghai, and the Hermitage Museum of St. Petersburg is doing likewise in London, Amsterdam, and Las Vegas. Is there any doubt that major museums have found new ways to globalize and to extract value from their well-known brands?

In the field of health, Abu Dhabi has arranged for a major cooperative agreement with the Cleveland Clinic. And most recently, New York University announced that it would establish a comprehensive liberal arts branch there by 2010.

Indeed, American universities are competing for global reach and presence into new territories like Singapore and India. The pace of these changes is staggering. Here's Tamar Lewin writing for the *New York Times* on Sunday, February 10, 2008 about higher education in another oil-rich Middle Eastern state, Qatar:

> Already students in Qatar can attend an American University without the expense, culture shock or post 9/11 problems of traveling to America. At Education City in Qatar they can study medicine at the Weill Medical College of Cornell University, science and business at Carnegie Mellon, fine art at Virginia Commonwealth, engineering at Texas A&M and soon, journalism at Northwestern.[4]

The globalization of nonprofits is fully upon us. Wise institutions and causes are asking how they can exploit their brand reputations overseas. They are leveraging the networks of university graduates and their wealthy parents and grateful former hospital patients as never before.

Even as arts, educational, and health institutions export their services, they arc importing philanthropy to strengthen their home bases and expand and enrich their missions.

PHILANTHROPIC CONVERTS BECOME PROSELYTIZERS

Closer to home, having acted so generously themselves, Warren Buffett and Bill Gates and their compatriots should join Ted Turner in urging others to open their minds, their hearts, and their pocketbooks to the charitable sector. It is not only an imperative of good leadership and good for one's tax profile, it is also fun, providing new meaning to the phrase "a life well led." Remember?

> He who gives
> When he lives
> Also knows
> Where it goes.

Peer pressure and influence, jawboning and preaching to the unconverted are needed in the for-profit sector, as well, if the potential for giving in America is to be tapped more fully.

UNDERPERFORMING BUSINESSES

Evidence abounds that America's natural resource firms—oil companies, coal companies, drilling and extraction outfits—are stinting when it comes to philanthropy. Although they are national firms with a global reach, outfits like Exxon-Mobil, Chevron, Newmont Mining, Freeport-McMoRan, and Halliburton tend to focus their contributions almost entirely in Dallas, San Francisco, Denver, Phoenix, and Houston, respectively, the cities in which they are headquartered. Notwithstanding zooming profits and a nationwide customer and shareholder base, none of these firms ranks high in this form of social responsibility elsewhere in America.

Curiously, investment firms that have moved over the last decade from partnerships to publicly held entities continue to run their philanthropy less as institutions than as aggregations of individuals. Measured against their net profits, the number of employees working in New York City and around the country, and all the benefits derived from being in Wall Street or elsewhere in Manhattan, their philanthropic output leaves plenty of room for improvement.

Compared, however, to leading hedge funds and private equity funds, investment firms are high performers.

Why Kohlberg Kravis Roberts, Blackstone, Texas Pacific, Carlyle, and other private equity firms do not do far more as collectivities for the Third Sector is a mystery even to their fans, such as Andrew Ross Sorkin, a financial reporter for the *New York Times*. It is true that many individuals in private equity such as Henry Kravis, Steve Schwartzman, David Rubenstein, and Russ Carson, to cite only a few, are philanthropically active and quite generous. But given the hundreds of deca- and centimillionaires employed by private equity funds and given the handsome tax breaks they enjoy, greater institutional support for charity would seem to be a form of sensible, enlightened self-interest.

The same observation applies with equal or greater force to the nation's leading hedge funds.

To be sure, what is called the alternative investment industry, encompassing hedge funds and private equity, is a fairly new institutional phenomenon. Hedge funds also enjoy outstanding philanthropic leaders like Bruce Kovner, Julian Robertson, Tom Lee and Paul Tudor Jones. But I think it is fair to state that these gentlemen are the exceptions that prove the following rule: compared to their funding capabilities, the performance of hedge funds philanthropically leaves a lot to be desired.

Properly encouraged by well informed, well connected, and highly motivated solicitors, and influenced by positive role models among their peers, over time these investment entities and those inside them can become new leaders in business philanthropy.

The part of the investment industry than can hold its head up high for outstanding results in philanthropy are money center banks like JPMorgan Chase & Co. and the Bank of New York Mellon Corporation. May their examples be widely emulated.[5]

If they are the leaders, then the laggards ought to be held to account by asking them for more, praising those who are responsive, and revealing the track record of all, for all to examine. In recent months, whole swaths of the investment industry, including hedge funds and private equity, have been battered. As they return to profitability over time, determining what obligations are owed to society and to the communities in which their employees live and work must be examined afresh. There remains in some quarters not just outright greed, but a general view that he who dies possessing the most toys wins.

Wins what? it may well be asked.

> Success, like happiness, cannot be pursued; it must ensue, and it only does so as the unintended side effect of one's dedication to a cause greater than oneself or as the by-product of one's surrender to a person other than oneself.[6]

In helping the philanthropically underperforming affluent and the firms that engage them to be more generous, in bringing to bear the wisdom of such wise men as Viktor Frankel writing in *Man's Search for Meaning*, truly we do them and their businesses, and not just our institutions and causes, a great favor. On the individual level, evidence grows that those who identify with causes beyond narrow self-interest tend to live longer and feel better about themselves. Arthur Brooks, a professor at Syracuse University, argues that givers of money and time are happier than nongivers. He reports that charitable activity induces endorphins that create a "high." They also lower the stress hormones that cause unhappiness.[7]

Similarly, at the institutional level, businesses with a reputation for demonstrably caring about the welfare of the communities in which their employees live and work are more likely to vie successfully for attracting and retaining talent and even to perform better financially than other less generous competitors.[8]

There are few less expensive or more joyful ways for individuals to live longer or better and for firms to thrive than to invest in institutions and causes that contribute to social welfare and that we care about as citizens, as parents, as taxpayers, and as employees.

E-PHILANTHROPY: UNREALIZED POTENTIAL

By the beginning of June 2008, candidate Barack Obama had raised about $265 million from well over 1.5 million political donors in his successful quest for the Democratic party nomination. Hillary Clinton fell behind, but collected the second highest total ever, $215 million, from an estimated 700,000 contributors. An unprecedented percentage of these financial supporters contributed online.

Only four years before, Howard Dean, then the rival of John Kerry for the Democratic nomination, was heralded as leading an Internet miracle. He raised a total of $51 million. How modest that sum looks today by comparison with the Obama and Clinton results!

In 2004, business-to-business sales of goods and services purchased over the Internet in America were estimated to exceed $1 trillion and online retail revenues were expected to reach $105 billion, or 50 percent of all U.S. retail spending in 2007, generated from 97 million customers.[9] Internet commerce has been growing in high double digits for at least the last decade.

By contrast, with politics and commerce, charitable gifts acquired over the Internet seem feeble.

Those institutions that do the best tend to be national, well known, and with broad-based appeal—such as the Nature Conservancy, Planned Parenthood, Care, Save the Children, and the Salvation Army.

When natural or man-made disasters suddenly strike—the tsunami that devastated Indonesia among other countries, the 9/11 attack on the United States, the genocide in Rwanda—Americans use the computer to contribute swiftly as befits the cause.

Although data about aggregate online gifts to charities is very sketchy, even as of 2007, they remain very small. However, 15 organizations raised more than $10 million online in 2006. Of those, 4 groups raised more than $40 million: the American Red Cross, the United Way of America, the American Cancer Society, and the Leukemia & Lymphoma Society.

When it comes to nonprofits, online giving is still in its infancy in both breadth and depth. In this area of fundraising, clearly the Third Sector needs to learn from the relative success of their political and profit-making counterparts.

Is the regularity of their communication by email to potential political donors and customers the secret to success?

Is it the simplicity and clarity of their sophisticated, demographically segmented message?

Is it the attractiveness of their sales pitch, often accompanied by full-motion video and easily retrievable photos and messages, that makes the difference?

We don't know. Plenty of experimentation is in order.

What we are sure of, however, is that Obama, Clinton, and companies like Amazon have professionals who specialize in e-giving and in e-commerce. They are digital experts. Commercial enterprises are filled with them. By comparison, in the realm of philanthropy, such posts are very few and far between.

Which of you are ready to adopt the lessons learned from politics and commerce to your fundraising challenge?

Who will make history by ushering the future through your open door?

Of course, success in exploiting Web-based technologies at first will supplement and, then, it is hoped, outpace direct mail and telemarketing as an entry-level method to attract donors. Paying assiduous attention to broadening the base of modest, newer donors, often called institutional members or friends, is essential. The larger and deeper the pool of lowest-level donors, the greater the opportunity to identify, then cultivate potential major gifts.

THINK BIG: IT'S A NEW MILLENNIUM

In dwelling on the future, do not neglect the possibility of the mega-, the übergift, one with the potential to transform an institution, or a program, or a cause.

Consider these acts of philanthropy:

- Eli Broad's decision to catapult the stalled fundraising for Walt Disney Concert Hall out of its decade-long doldrums with a galvanizing gift of $10 million and a pledge to rally others to the cause until the now-heralded Frank Gehry landmark was constructed. He moved the project to success with a sense of civic urgency.

- John Kluge's $450 million to Columbia University for student scholarships.

- The hundreds of millions of dollars of support from George Soros to the fledgling nonprofit and advocacy organizations blossoming throughout Eastern Europe, particularly after the fall of the Berlin Wall in 1989.

- Mort Zuckerman's $100 million to Memorial Sloan-Kettering Hospital, insuring that its building expansion program happens in timely fashion.

- Mayor Michael Bloomberg's pledge of $125 million to reduce smoking worldwide, thereby decreasing rates of mortality, a stunning initiative to do outside New York City so much of what was accomplished inside.

- David Rockefeller's $100 million unrestricted gift to the Museum of Modern Art, the last of his many to MoMA.

- The billions of dollars committed by Melinda and Bill Gates to the prevention and treatment of AIDS, malaria, and tuberculosis, particularly on the continent of Africa.

These stunning donations hold promise of being transformational for the institutions that received them or for the causes they are intended to advance.

What makes these illustrative huge gifts possible is unprecedented levels of affluence.

Such extreme wealth, known to so many, has never before existed in history. It is a difference of degree in personal fortunes so large as to have become a difference of kind.

In the context of your institution's size and aspiration, who are your potential megadonors?

Are they in your sights and on your mind?

They should be.

After all, their generosity is yours for the asking.

CHAPTER 10

QUOTATIONS THAT MATTER

Raising money for a nonprofit institution or cause is more than a job. It is a privilege. It is an act of nobility. It is a calling.

Too often fundraisers forget how moving is their vocation, how rooted in universal values, whether religiously inspired or otherwise.

It has been frequently observed that, during the years of the Bush administration, the American people were never asked by their government to sacrifice. While war was waged in Iraq, soldiers and their families carried an exclusively heavy burden. They were not joined by an American people paying higher taxes or participating in some form of national service in a period of armed conflict.

There is a yearning in America to contribute to something larger than self or family, to make an impact, leave an impression, help those in need or simply less fortunate than most of us. Building institutions, fostering movements, inventing new ways to solve problems—these are exciting, energizing activities. Undertaking missions like relief of suffering, reducing poverty, preventing disease and improving education are all very special. They offer as much or more to the contributor than they do to the so-called beneficiary.

The quotations that follow alphabetically by author remind us why it is worth the effort to help others and build a more just society. They help us recall how the habit of giving is centuries old and respects no geographic, ethnic, or religious boundary.

To give and to ask is as human an endeavor as deep breathing and exercise. We should engage in them more often. They are excellent for our health and for the welfare of the communities we call home and the businesses that are our places of work.

He who throws mud, loses ground.

—Anonymous

Noah's principle says: No more credit for predicting rain; credit only for building arks.

—Anonymous

One gives generously and ends with more.
Another stints on doing right and incurs a loss.

—Anonymous

The weakest ink is more powerful than the strongest memory.

—Anonymous

To give away money is an easy matter in
any man's power. But to decide to whom
to give it, and how large and when, and
for what purpose and how, is neither
in every man's power nor an easy matter.

—Aristotle, *Nicomachean Ethics*

The life of money-making is one undertaken under compulsion, and wealth is evidently not the good we are seeking, for it is merely useful for the sake of something else.

—Aristotle, *Nicomachean Ethics*

We invest in our communities for a very simple reason.
We live here too.

—Bank of America

We expect the rich to be generous with their wealth, and criticize them when they are not; but when they make benefactions, we question their motives, deplore the method by which they obtained their abundance, and wonder whether their gifts will not do more harm than good.

—**Robert Bremmer**, *American Philanthropy*

He who gives
While he lives
Also knows
Where it goes

—**Eli Broad**, quoting an anonymous source

Listening, not imitation, maybe the sincerest form of flattery. . . . If you want to influence someone, listen to what he says.

—**Dr. Joyce Brothers**

Anything not worth doing well is not worth doing.

—**Warren Buffett**

A man there was, tho' some count him mad
The more he cast away, the more he had
He that bestows his Goods upon the Poor
Shall have as much again, and ten times more.

—**John Bunyan**, *The Pilgrim's Progress*

. . . the day is not far distant when the man who dies leaving behind him millions of available wealth, which was free for him to administer during life, will pass away unwept, unhonored, and unsung.

—**Andrew Carnegie**, *The Gospel of Wealth*

He who dies rich, dies disgraced.

—**Andrew Carnegie**, *The Gospel of Wealth*

Surplus wealth is a sacred trust which its possessor is bound to administer in his lifetime for the good of the community.

—**Andrew Carnegie**

This, then, is held to be the duty of the man of wealth: First, to set an example of modest, unostentatious living, shunning display or extravagance: to provide moderately for the legitimate wants of those dependent upon him; and, after doing so, to consider all surplus revenues which come to him simply as trust funds . . . Which he is strictly bound as a matter of duty to administer in the manner which, in his judgment, is both calculated to provide the most beneficial results for the community—the man of wealth thus becoming the mere trustee and agent for his poorer brethren.

—Andrew Carnegie, *The Gospel of Wealth*

My popularity, my happiness and source of worth depend to no small extent upon my skill in dealing with people.

—Dale Carnegie

Many a man would rather you heard his story than granted his request.

—Lord Chesterfield

If it can be imagined
It can be done.
This is America.
We never say good enough.
We never say die.

—The CIT Group

And now abideth faith, hope, charity,
these three; but the greatest of these
[is] charity.

—I Corinthians 13:13

It is not the strongest of the species that survive, nor the most intelligent, but the most responsive to change.

—**Anonymous** (often mistakenly attributed to Charles Darwin)

By my works I will show you my faith.

—Epistle of James

Most people buy not because they believe, but because the salesman believes.

—Ben Feldman

Dare to be naïve.

—Buckminster Fuller

Success, like happiness, cannot be pursued; it must ensue, and it only does so as the unintended side effect of one's dedication to a cause greater than oneself or as the by-product of one's surrender to a person other than oneself.

—Viktor E. Frankl, *Man's Search for Meaning*

In the first place, I advise you to apply to all those you know will give you something, next to those whom you are uncertain whether they will give you anything or not and show them the list of those who have given and lastly, do not neglect those whom you are sure will give you nothing, for in some of them, you will be mistaken.

—Benjamin Franklin, *The Autobiography of Benjamin Franklin*

The defining and ongoing innovations of this age—biotechnology, the computer, the Internet—give us a chance we've never had before to end extreme poverty and death from preventable disease . . .
   Members of the Harvard Family: Here in the Yard is one of the great collections of intellectual talent in the world.
What for?

—Bill Gates, Harvard commencement address

You must be the change you wish to see in the world.

—Mahatma Gandhi

The difference between what we do and what we are capable of doing would suffice to solve most of the world's problems.

—Mahatma Gandhi

People don't lack strength; they lack will.

—Victor Hugo

Unto whomsoever much is given, of him shall much be required, and to whom men have committed much, of him they will ask for more.

—Jesus

There was a kind lady called Gregory
said, "Come to me, poets in beggary."
But found her imprudence
when thousands of students
cried, "all, we are all in that category."

—James Joyce, limerick written to his patron, Lady Gregory

It is from the numberless diverse acts of courage and belief that human history is shaped. Each time a man stands up for an ideal, or acts to improve the lot of others, or strikes out against injustice, he sends a tiny ripple of hope, and crossing each other from a million different centers of energy and daring, those ripples build a current which can sweep down the mightiest walls of oppression and resistance.

—Robert Kennedy, from a speech given in South Africa

The fierce urgency of now . . .

—Martin Luther King, Jr., from the speech Beyond Vietnam

Life is not primarily a quest for pleasure, as Freud believed, or a quest for power, as Alfred Adler taught, but a quest for meaning.

—Harold S. Kushner, Foreword to Viktor E. Frankl's Man's Search for Meaning, (2006 edition)

You may say I'm a dreamer,
but I'm not the only one.

—John Lennon, from the song Imagine

You don't raise major gifts by postage stamps. You do it by shoe leather.

—Naomi Levine

With malice toward none; with charity for all; with firmness on the right, as God gives us to see the right.

—**Abraham Lincoln**, second inaugural address,

He who persuades others to give alms and moves them to act thus, his reward is greater that the reward of him who gives alms himself.

—Maimonides

Ladder of Charity

Responsibility
At the top of the ladder is the gift of self-reliance.
To hand someone a gift or a loan, or to enter into a partnership with him, or to find work for him, so that he will never have to beg again.

Anonymity
To give to someone you don't know, and to do so anonymously.

Corruption
To give to someone you know, but who doesn't know from whom he is receiving help.

Boundaries
To give to someone you don't know, but allow your name to be known.

Shame
To hand money to the poor before being asked, but risk making the recipient feel shame.

Solicitation
To hand money to the poor after being asked.

Proportion
To give less to the poor than is proper, but to do so cheerfully.

Reluctance
To give begrudgingly.

—Maimonides

Dig your well before you're thirsty.

—**Harvey Mackay**, *Dig Your Well Before You're Thirsty*

A wise man should ever follow the ways of great men . . .

He should do as the skillful archer, who, seeing that the object he desires to hit is too distant . . . aims higher than the destined mark.

—Niccolo Machiavelli, *The Prince*

For it is the nature of men to be bound by the benefits they confer as much as by those they receive.

—Niccolo Machiavelli, *The Prince*

There is nothing more difficult to take in hand, more perilous to conduct, or more uncertain in its success, than to take the lead in the introduction of a new order of things.

—Niccolo Machiavelli, *The Prince*

My favorite optimist was an American who jumped off the Empire State Building and, as he passed the 42nd floor, the window washer heard him say, "So far, so good."

—John McGahern

My country has been invaded and it's very possible we can be pushed into the sea. If your grandparents had turned left instead of right, you'd be living in my country [Israel]. Now we need your help. I don't have the time for you to go home and think about it. I don't have the time for you to consult with your tax advisors. I don't have the time to leave it in your will. I need it now.

—Golda Meier (as remembered by John Rosenwald; $300 million was raised in response to this appeal in the immediate aftermath of the start of the Yom Kippur War)

In necessary things, unity; in doubtful things, Liberty; in all things charity.

—Rupertus Meldenius

Nothing is possible without men; nothing is lasting without institutions.

—Jean Monnet, *Memoirs*

Do what you can, with what you have, where you are.

—Theodore Roosevelt

Shall we devote the few precious days of our existence only to buying and selling, only to comparing sales with the sales of the same day the year before, only to shuffling our feet in the dance, only to matching little picture cards so as to group together three jacks or aces or Kings, only to seek pleasures and fight taxes, and when the end comes to leave as little taxable an estate as possible as the final triumph and achievement of our lives? Surely there is something finer and better in life, something that dignifies it and stamps it with at least some little touch of the divine.

My friends it is unselfish effort, helpfulness to others, that ennobles life, not because of what it does for others but more what it does for ourselves. In this spirit, we should give not grudgingly, not niggardly, but gladly, generously, eagerly, lovingly, joyfully, indeed with the supremest pleasure that life can furnish.

—Julius Rosenwald

It is nearly always easier to earn one million dollars honestly than to dispose of it wisely.

—Julius Rosenwald

Treat donors gently, respond thoughtfully to their requests, and let them know that they are very important people, because they are.

—Henry Rosso, *Rosso on Fund Raising*

He profits most who serves the best.

—A Rotary Club Motto

In the end we are not measured by what we have, but by what we give to one another.

—Julie Salamon, *Rambam's Ladder*

Everyone has his own patch of earth to cultivate.
What's important is that he dig deep.

—José Saramago

It is certainly not a good citizen who does not wish to promote, by every means in his power, the welfare of the whole society of his fellow citizens.

—**Adam Smith,** *The Theory of Moral Sentiments*

How selfish so ever man may be supposed, there are evidently some principles of his nature, which interest him in the fortunes of others, and render their happiness necessary to him, though he derives nothing from it, except the pleasure of seeing it.

—**Adam Smith,** *The Theory of Moral Sentiments*

Every individual endeavors to employ his capital so that its produce may be of greatest value. . . . He intends only his own security, only his own gain. . . . By pursuing his interest he frequently promotes that of society more effectively than when he really intends to promote it.

—**Adam Smith,** *The Wealth of Nations*

You cannot win if you're not at the table. You have to be where the action is.

—**Ben Stein,** University of Miami spring convocation address

It is not required of thee to complete the task, but neither art thou free to desist therefrom. . . . He who saves one life, it is as if he has saved the whole world.

—**The Talmud**

Philanthropy is America's passing gear.

—**Paul Ylvisaker**

We are the ones we've been waiting for. We are the ones, my friends, we've been waiting for. Let's now start doing the job.

—**Old Gospel Song**

BIBLIOGRAPHY

One of the most creative challenges of raising money for your favorite cause or organization is figuring out how to interest and motivate your prospect.

Doing so is not just a matter of learning all you can about the personal or institutional history of a potential donor. Knowing where he or she was raised, attended school, and earns a living is critical. Understanding the family background—parents, siblings, and children—who they are, where they came from, what interests them—is helpful. Identifying your possible benefactor's values and passions is utterly necessary.

The same observation applies to institutional donors: foundations and corporations. What are their guidelines for applicants? What is their history? Who are the real decision makers? How can you become better acquainted with them and appeal to their preferences?

Beyond the detailed research from public data sources and from those familiar with the donors you are endeavoring to engage, there is literature with which you should be well acquainted.

If your targets are corporations or business executives and those who serve them, or buy and sell their stock, or bring them to market—hedge fund, mutual fund and private equity managers, investment bankers, lawyers—then you should be fully acquainted with what they read: *The American Lawyer, Barron's, Business Week,* the *Financial Times, Forbes, Fortune,* the *Harvard Business Review, Institutional Investor,* the *New York Times,* the *Wall Street Journal,* and company annual reports, among other publications.

No matter the organization or cause on whose behalf one labors, certain sources of literature are required reading: the *Chronicle of Philanthropy, Corporate Philanthropy Reports,* the *Foundation News, Giving USA,* and the *Nonprofit Times* all fall into this category.

Of course, each field—the arts, higher education, health, social services, the environment, housing, the humanities, and primary and secondary schools education—has its own specialized newspapers, periodicals, and trade publications with which you must become familiar. And the annual reports of corporate foundations and private foundations are also must reading.

Donors respect fundraisers who have done their homework. They enjoy responding to informed questions about themselves and their places of work. They think highly of the intellectually and socially curious, the widely read, the solicitor who has troubled to learn what the prospect is really about.

Beyond the daily newspapers and the weekly and monthly periodicals, there are books well worth digesting. They will help you navigate through the institutions that are your natural habitats. They will help you create an intellectual context for your work, familiarizing you with the history, the economics, the sociology, the psychology, and the politics of the organizations from which you seek funds. Visit their Web sites as well. They will provide valuable information about the organization and its priorities.

Other books will acquaint you with the skills and techniques regularly brought to the fundraising vocation.

In what follows, I offer a list of books, a bibliography, I have found extremely worthwhile to devour and repair to, sometimes quite often. Raising funds is often a lonely task. Colleagues are reluctant to share information. How things are done frequently occurs behind closed doors. Too frequently you'll find yourself on the wrong side of them.

Under such circumstances, the library you develop can be not only a valuable asset but a shortcut to the actionable intelligence that otherwise only hard-won experience can provide.

Abshire, Michael, ed. *Giving by Industry: A Reference Guide to the New Corporate Philanthropy*. Gaithersburg, MD: Aspen Publishers, 2001.

Bellah, Robert N. et al. *Habits of the Heart: Individualism and Commitment in American Life*. Berkeley: University of California Press, 1985.

Brawer, Robert A. *Fictions of Business: Insights on Management from Great Literature*. New York: John Wiley & Sons, Inc., 1998.

Bremner, Robert H. *American Philanthropy*, 2nd ed. Chicago: University of Chicago Press, 1988.

   Giving: Charity and Philanthropy in History. New Brunswick, NJ: Transaction, 1994.

Brooks, Arthur C. *Who Really Cares: America's Charity Divide: Who Gives, Who Doesn't and Why It Matters.* New York: Basic Books, 2006.

Burlingame, Dwight F., and Lamont J. Hulse, eds. *Taking Fund Raising Seriously.* San Francisco: Jossey-Bass, 1991.

Burlingame, Dwight F., and Dennis R. Young, eds. *Corporate Philanthropy at the Crossroads.* Bloomington: Indiana University Press, 1996.

Carnegie, Dale. *How to Win Friends and Influence People.* New York: Simon and Schuster, 1936.

Currid, Elizabeth. *The Warhol Economy: How Fashion, Art and Music Drive New York City.* Princeton, NJ: Princeton University Press, 2007.

Damon, William and Susan Verducci, eds. *Taking Philanthropy Seriously: Beyond Noble Intentions to Responsible Giving.* Bloomington: Indiana University Press, 2006.

Danziger, Danny. *Museum: Behind the Scenes at the Metropolitan Museum of Art.* New York: Viking, 2007.

Drucker, Peter F. *Managing the Nonprofit Organization: Principles and Practices.* New York: HarperCollins, 1990.

Managing for Results. London: Pan Books, 1984.

Fisher, Roger, and William Ury. *Getting to Yes: Negotiating Agreement Without Giving In.* New York: Penguin Books, 1991.

Fleishman, Joel L. *The Foundation: A Great American Secret: How Private Wealth Is Changing the World.* New York: Public Affairs, 2007.

Frankl, Victor E. *Man's Search for Meaning.* Boston: Beacon Press, 2006.

Gardner, John W. *Excellence.* New York: Harper and Brothers, 1961.

Gardner, John W. *Self-Renewal: The Individual and the Innovative Society.* New York: W. W. Norton, 1981.

Gregorian, Vartan. *The Road to Home: My Life and Times.* New York: Simon and Schuster, 2003.

Grossman, Allen et al. *High-Performance Nonprofit Organizations: Managing Upstream for Greater Impact.* New York: John Wiley & Sons, Inc., 1999.

Hodgkinson. Virginia A., and Richard Wibyman, eds. *The Future of the Non-profit Sector.* San Francisco: Jossey-Bass, 1989.

Ilchman, Warren F., Stanley Katz, and Edward L. Queen II. *Philanthropy in the World's Traditions.* Bloomington: Indiana University Press, 1998.

Karoff, Peter, and Jane Maddox. *The World We Want: New Dimensions in Philanthropy and Social Change*. New York: Ata Mira Press, 2008.

Lagemann, Ellen Confliffe. *Philanthropic Foundations: New Scholarship, New Possibilities*. Indianapolis: Indiana University Press, 1999.

Levy, Reynold. *Give and Take: A Candid Account of Corporate Philanthropy*. Cambridge, MA: Harvard Business School Press, 1999.

Matthews, Chris. *Life's a Campaign: What Politics Has Taught Me about Friendship, Rivalry, Reputation and Success*. New York: Random House, 2007.

Nielsen, Waldemar A. *The Big Foundations*. New York: Columbia University Press, 1972.

    The Endangered Sector. New York: Columbia University, 1972.

    The Golden Donors: A New Anatomy of the Great Foundations. New York: E. P. Dutton, 1989.

    Inside American Philanthropy: The Dramas of Donorship. Norman, OK: University of Oklahoma Press, 1996.

Novak, Michael. *Business as a Calling: Work and the Examined Life*. New York: The Free Press, 1996.

O'Connell, Brian, ed. *America's Voluntary Spirit: A Book of Readings*. New York: Foundation Center, 1983.

Odendahl, Teresa, ed. *America's Wealthy and the Future of Foundations*. New York: Foundation Center, 1987.

O'Neill, Michael. *The Third America*. San Francisco: Jossey-Bass, 1989.

Ostrower, Francis. *Why the Wealthy Give: The Culture of Elite Philanthropy*. Princeton, NJ: Princeton University Press, 1995.

Payton, Robert L. *Philanthropy: Voluntary Action for the Public Good*. New York: Macmillan, 1988.

Peale, Norman Vincent. *The Power of Positive Thinking*. New York: Prentice-Hall, Inc., 1952.

Prince, Russ Alan, and Lewis Schiff. *The Middle-Class Millionaire: The Rise of the New Rich and How They Are Changing America*. New York: Doubleday, 2008.

Rosenberg, Claude N. *Wealthy and Wise: How You and America Can Get the Most Out of Your Giving*. New York: Little, Brown & Company, 1994.

Rosovsky, Henry. *The University: An Owner's Manual*. New York: W. W. Norton and Company, 1990.

Salamon, Julie. *Rambam's Ladder: A Meditation on Generosity and Why It Is Necessary to Give*. New York: Workman Publishing, 2003.

Salamon, Lester M. *America's Nonprofit Sector: A Primer*. New York: Foundation Center, 1982.

Salamon, Lester M., ed. *The State of Nonprofit America*. Washington, DC: Brookings Institution Press, 2002.

Schervish, Paul G., ed. *Taking Giving Seriously*. Indianapolis: Indiana University Center on Philanthropy, 1993.

Shannon, James P., ed. *The Corporate Contributions Handbook*. San Francisco: Jossey-Bass, 1991.

Shore, Bill. *The Cathedral Within: Transforming Your Life by Giving Something Back*. New York: Random House, 1999.

Simons, Robin, and Richard Steckel. *Doing Best by Doing Good: How to Use Public Purpose Partnerships to Boost Corporate Profits and Benefit Your Community*. New York: Dutton, 1992.

Stanley, Thomas J., and William D. Danko. *The Millionaire Next Door: The Surprising Secrets of America's Wealthy*. Atlanta: Longstreet Press, 1996.

Wandroff, Alan L., and Kay Sprankel Grace. *High-Impact Philanthropy*. Hoboken, NJ: John Wiley & Sons, Inc., 2007.

Weisbrod, Burton A. *The Nonprofit Economy*. Cambridge, MA: Harvard University Press, 1988.

Wolf, Thomas. *Managing a Nonprofit Organization in the Twenty-First Century*. New York: Simon and Schuster, 1999.

Wolpert, Julian. *Patterns of Generosity in America: Who's Holding the Safety Net*. New York: Twentieth Century Fund, 1993.

Wuthnow, Robert. *Acts of Compassion: Caring for Others and Helping Ourselves*. Princeton, NJ: Princeton University Press, 1991.

  Learning to Care: Elementary Kindness in an Age of Indifference. New York: Oxford University Press, 1995.

  Poor Richard's Principle: Rediscovering the American Dream Through the Moral Dimension of Work, Business and Money. Princeton, NJ: Princeton University Press, 1996.

FUNDRAISING ON STEROIDS: LINCOLN CENTER

In this appendix, you will find Lincoln Center Capital Campaign Donors, listed according to amount donated. You may also review two exhibits detailing the change in funding landscape from FY 2002 through FY 2008 (Exhibit A.1) and the total Lincoln Center funds raised from FY2002 through FY 2008 (Exhibit A.2).

EXHIBIT **A.1** *Change in Funding Landscape FY 2002–2008*

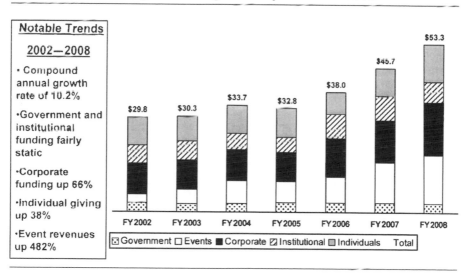

EXHIBIT **A.2**   *Lincoln Center Funds Raised FY 2002–FY 2008*

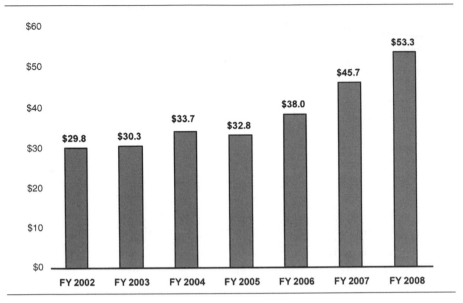

Bravo Lincoln Center: Capital Campaign Donors

Bravo Champion
($20,000,000 and above)

The City of New York

The State of New York

Federal Highway Administration and Federal Transit Administration

Bruce and Suzie Kovner

Ronald P. Stanton

The Starr Foundation

Bravo Benefactor
($10,000,000 and above)

Ford Foundation

Laurie M. Tisch Illumination Fund

The Alice Tully Foundation

One Anonymous

Bravo Patron
($5,000,000 and above)

The Robert A. and Renée E. Belfer Family Foundation

The Carson Family Charitable Trust

Citi Foundation

Jerome L. Greene Foundation, Inc.

The Hauser Foundation

The Hearst Foundations and Hearst Corporation

Hess Corporation

Hess Foundation, Inc.

The Andrew W. Mellon Foundation

Morgan Stanley

Josie and Julian H. Robertson, Jr.

Kara and Stephen M. Ross

Alice and David Rubenstein

The Peter Jay Sharp Foundation

Ziff Family

One Anonymous

Bravo Partner
($3,000,000 and above)

The Bank of New York Mellon Foundation

Credit Suisse

The Walt Disney Company

Anne and Joel Ehrenkranz

Katherine Farley and Jerry I. Speyer

Roslyn and Elliot Jaffe Family

JPMorgan

William R. Kenan, Jr. Charitable Trust

Lehman Brothers

Betty and John Levin

Mr. and Mrs. Peter L. Malkin

Merrill Lynch

Charles H. Revson Foundation, Inc.

Barbara and Donald Zucker

Two Anonymous

Bravo Sustainer
($1,000,000 and above)

AIG

American Express

Mary Lake and Frank A. Bennack, Jr.

Mr. and Mrs. James A. Block

Charina Endowment Fund/Horace W. Goldsmith Foundation

Deutsche Bank

Cheryl and Blair Effron

Frieda and Roy Furman

Goldman Sachs

Harvey and Roberta Golub

Leonard Lauder

Thomas H. Lee and Ann Tenenbaum

Macy's Inc.

McKinsey & Company

Cheryl and Philip Milstein

The Ambrose Monell Foundation

Edward John Noble Foundation, Inc.

Omnicom

The Pasculano Foundation

PepsiCo Foundation

Amy and Joseph Perella

Polo Ralph Lauren

Ingeborg and Ira Leon Rennert

David Rockefeller

Susan and Jon Rotenstreich

The Fan Fox and Leslie R. Samuels Foundation, Inc.

Paul and Daisy Soros

Jonathan Tisch

Bruce and Robbi Toll

Turner Construction Company

UBS

Verizon

Mildred and George Weissman

Bravo Friend
($500,000 and above)
Altria Group, Inc.
Richard and Susan Braddock
Nancy A. Marks
Leni and Peter May
Nicki and Harold Tanner

Bravo Leader
($100,000 and above)
The Achelis Foundation
The Bodman Foundation
Booth Ferris Foundation
Chris and Bruce Crawford
Jennie L. and Richard K. DeScherer
Ernst & Young LLP
Barry S. Friedberg and
Charlotte Moss
Bart Friedman and Wendy A. Stein
Efraim Grinberg
Arthur Hershaft
David and Alice Hunt
Frayda and George Lindemann
Leonard Litwin
Sir Deryck and Lady Va Maughan
Raymond J. McGuire
Mitsui USA
William C. and Susan F. Morris
The Morse Family Foundation
Movado
The New York Community Trust
The Rebell Family

Heidi and Stefan Selig
Mr. and Mrs. Howard Solomon
Ambassador Carl Spielvogel and
Barbaralee Diamonstein
Wachovia Foundation
John C. Whitehead
Janice Savin Williams and
Christopher J. Williams
One Anonymous

Bravo Supporter
(Up to $99,999)
Norma Asnes
Susan Baker and Michael Lynch
Carolyn and Laurence Belfer
Elizabeth Belfer
Mr. and Mrs. Albert C. Bellas
Diane M. Coffey
Jean S. and Richard E. Deems
Peter Frelinghuysen
Louis V. Gerstner
Diane and Paul Guenther
Gurnee F. Hart
Ruth Houghton
Landmark West!
Nathan Leventhal
Elizabeth Cooke and Reynold Levy
Bertha and Isaac Liberman
Foundation
The Fay J. Lindner Foundation
John B. Madden
Shelly and Tony Malkin

William F. May

Monterey Fund, Inc.

Martin J. Oppenheimer

Mrs. Lisa Schiff

Roberta and Irwin Schneiderman

Edith and Martin E. Segal

Esther Simon Charitable Trust

The John R. and Inge P. Stafford Foundation

Strong Foundation of New York

Julien J. Studley

Time Equities, Inc.

Alair A. Townsend

NONPROFIT BOARD OF DIRECTORS SIZE: A NATIONAL SAMPLER AND LINCOLN CENTER

Nonprofit Board of Directors: Size Matters	
INSTITUTION	*2007*
The Arena Stage	56
The Art Institute of Chicago	40
The Berkeley Repertory Theater	35
Carnegie Hall	73
The Carnival Center	78
The Cleveland Hospital (Clinic)	102
The Cleveland Symphony	90
The Kennedy Center	137*
LACMA (The Los Angeles County Art Museum)	57
Lincoln Center for the Performing Arts	68
The Los Angeles Symphony	53
The Manhattan Theater Club	42
The Massachusetts General Hospital	20
Mount Sinai Hospital	72

(*Continued*)

INSTITUTION	2007
The Museum of Natural History	103
New School University	56
New York/Columbia Presbyterian Hospital	108
The Philadelphia Orchestra	75
The Phoenix Museum	51
The San Francisco Ballet	88
The San Francisco Symphony	100
Sloan Kettering Hospital	64
The Tyrone Guthrie Theater	75
The University of Chicago	97
The University of Wisconsin at Madison	17

*Includes presidential appointments and ex-officio trustees.

Lincoln Center's Component Organizations: Board Size

INSTITUTION	2007
The Chamber Music Society of Lincoln Center	21
The Film Society of Lincoln Center, Inc.	41
Jazz at Lincoln Center	39
The Juilliard School	28
The Library for the Performing Arts	70
The Lincoln Center Corporate Fund Leadership Committee	33
Lincoln Center for the Performing Arts	68
Lincoln Center Theater	43
The Metropolitan Opera	44
The New York City Ballet	44
The New York City Opera	41
The New York Philharmonic	52
The School of American Ballet	48

APPENDIX III

Governance at Lincoln Center: 2007

COMMITTEE (NUMBER OF MEETINGS)	COMMITTEE CHAIR
Art Committee (1)	Donald Marron
Audit Committee (2)	Alair A. Townsend
Board of Directors (3)	Frank A. Bennack, Jr.
Bond Financing Task Force (1)	Richard K. DeScherer
Campaign Steering Committee (2)	David M. Rubenstein
Campus-Wide Marketing Committee (4)	Richard S. Braddock
Chairman's Council (4)	Frank A. Bennack, Jr.
Counsels' Council/Legal Committee (2)	Bart Friedman
Development Committee (4)	Roy L. Furman
Education Committee/LCI Board (5)	Susan Rudin
Executive Committee (6)	Frank A. Bennack
50th Anniversary Committee (2)	Ann Ziff, Tom Renyi
Finance Committee (3)	Joel S. Ehrenkranz
General Services Committee (2)	Julien J. Studley
Harmony Atrium Task Force (5)	Philip L. Milstein
Investment Committee (3)	Harvey Golub
New Media Committee (1)	David A. Hunt
New Ventures Committee (1)	David A. Hunt
Nominating and Governance Committee (4)	Thomas H. Lee

(*Continued*)

COMMITTEE (NUMBER OF MEETINGS)	COMMITTEE CHAIR
Presidents' Council (4)	Reynold Levy
Public Affairs Committee (2)	Blair W. Effron
Restaurant Task Force (4)	Robert A. Alexander
Steering Committee for the Corporate Fund (2)	William B. Harrison
Lincoln Center Development Project (LCDP) (13)	Katherine Farley
LCDP Audit Committee (3)	Susan Baker
LCDP Board of Directors (2)	Katherine Farley
LCDP Building Advisory Group (3)	Daniel Brodsky
LCDP Promenade Project Working Group (2)	Daniel Brodsky
65th Street Project Working Group (3)	Bruce Kovner

THREE DIRECT MAIL HOME RUNS FROM THE INTERNATIONAL RESCUE COMMITTEE

PAUL NEWMAN

Dear Friend,

It is impossible to be unmoved by the plight of refugees who so often appear on our television screens and in our newspapers these days.

Their suffering compels us to examine our own humanity and choose compassionate action over indifference.

I ask you to join me in supporting the International Rescue Committee, which focuses exclusively on providing refugees worldwide with life-saving, hope-giving assistance.

Whether it is women and children forced to search for clean water in the face of conflict and chaos in Darfur, Sudan . . . an Indonesian child huddled in a threadbare tent after her home was destroyed by an earthquake . . . or families separated during Liberia's devastating wars . . . the International Rescue Committee offers emergency aid—and a beacon of hope amid crushing despair—to refugees in need.

Compelling evidence of the importance of the International Rescue Committee's work, and why your support is so urgently needed, can be found all around our troubled world . . .

. . . in the hundreds of places where innocent men, women, and children have been forced to flee violence, ethnic, religious or political persecution, civil war, and domestic unrest—and are plunged into a desperate struggle for survival.

Consider the situation in Darfur, Sudan as just one example. As I write you today, the International Rescue Committee is one of the few organizations able to reach refugees who have been driven from their homes by murderous militias.

It is estimated that over 300,000 people have died in Darfur at the hands of vicious armed mercenaries that have raped and killed, burned entire villages, and sent the survivors—mostly women and children—fleeing for their lives. Over two million people have been displaced so far.

For several years, the IRC has been on the ground, working tirelessly to save lives. The IRC is running the only health clinic tending to patients' needs 24 hours a day, and bringing services and support to victims of sexual violence—critically important in a society still reluctant to acknowledge the crime of rape.

It's an enormous task, and one that is testing the International Rescue Committee's ability to save the lives of the innocent as never before.

That's why I am urging you to rush a tax-deductible donation of $20, $35, $50, or a bit more if you are able, in the enclosed envelope. No matter how much you can help, your immediate reply is essential because the humanitarian crisis in Darfur is not the only one now being addressed by the International Rescue Committee.

The continuing struggle of refugees returning to Afghanistan has been pushed off the evening news, but the International Rescue Committee is still there helping restore some sense of normalcy and hope for a secure, self-sufficient future. Likewise, the IRC has not abandoned Liberian civilians imperiled by food shortages, disease outbreaks, and ongoing violence. International Rescue Committee relief workers are on the scene fighting hunger, disease, and despair—helping families regain their sense of safety and the abilit to fend for themselves.

These are just a few examples of where and how the IRC comes to the aid of refugees worldwide—you can learn more in the enclosed newsletter or by visiting the IRC Web site, www.theIRC.org.

But I hope you can see why your support is so urgently needed.

Nonetheless, before answering my request, you probably want evidence that your support will make a real difference. On that score, you don't have to take my word for it.

Publications such as *Newsweek, Consumers Digest, SmartMoney*, and *Forbes* magazines have repeatedly ranked the International Recue Committee as one of America's top charities. *SmartMoney* even says donors "get the most bang for your donated buck" by supporting the IRC.

That's because more than 90 cents of every dollar the IRC spends goes directly to helping refugees.

Charity watchdog groups give the IRC high marks for fiscal efficiency as well. The American Institute for Philanthropy gives the IRC an "A+." And the International Rescue Committee meets all the standards set for charities by the Better Business Bureau's Wise Giving Alliance.

So if you have ever been moved by the plight of refugees who share our basic humanity—but not the same sense of security—and wondered what you could do to help them, I urge you to join me in supporting the International Rescue Committee.

There are moments in all our lives when a decision to act with compassion in response to immense tragedy takes the measure of our humanity. Refugee crises in so many parts of our troubled world make this one of those times.

Please confirm my fondest hope that you are up to the test by giving the International Rescue Committee your support.

Thank you, in advance, for responding as quickly and generously as possible.

Best Regards,

Paul Newman

P.S. I have played a variety of roles over the years, but none has been as important and personally rewarding as the real-life role I play as a supporter of the International Rescue Committee.

TOM BROKAW, COCHAIR, BOARD OF OVERSEERS

Dear Friend,

When we turn to an organization to help people whose lives are literally hanging in the balance, it's not enough to know that it has good intentions. We need to know that it has the experience and the ability to act on those good intentions.

From personal experience I know the International Rescue Committee passes that test with flying colors. In some of the most difficult, life-and-death situations in the world, the IRC acts with incredible skill, conviction, and courage.

And today, I'm hoping you will act as well by offering a measure of support to this remarkable organization.

When I go on assignment to the world's trouble spots, I often discover the IRC there ahead of me. No matter how dangerous the territory or how difficult the work, the IRC is already on the ground rescuing refugees caught in crisis.

I am mindful of the fact that everywhere I saw the skill and compassion of the IRC at work, I was witnessing the impact of the personal generosity of individual IRC supporters—people who were willing to step forward and help the IRC rescue refugees and displaced people who are running out of time—and running out of hope.

I am writing today to urge you to step forward.

With your help, the IRC can rescue people trapped in the ongoing crises in earthquake-ravaged Pakistan, Chechnya, and the raging conflicts in Uganda and the Democratic Republic of Congo. IRC workers are spending long nights and days assisting refugees in Sudan's Darfur region. And they remain at work in the tsunami zone. Those are just a few of the places where the IRC is at work. In each and every one of them, your decision to act can have an immediate live-saving impact.

That's because the IRC acts at the point of emergency, rescuing people who have been driven from their homes by war and political upheaval—and responding to natural disasters that, all too frequently, strike while IRC is already on the ground.

And here at home, when Hurricane Katrina dealt a devastating blow to the people of the Gulf Coast region, the IRC was called upon to immediately lend its expertise to helping evacuees rebuild their lives.

If I seem to be writing about the IRC in very personal terms, there is a reason. You see, the Brokaw family has a long history with this remarkable organization. It dates from my daughter's work in Europe helping refugees from Soviet oppression to her six months in Pakistan, providing health care to Afghani women during the Soviet occupation.

Jennifer saw this legendary organization from the inside and impressed on the rest of our family the importance of the IRC's work. So when I was given the opportunity to take on a new role with the IRC, I quickly agreed. Jennifer's engagement with the IRC has continued as well. A highly-skilled physician, she was a member of the IRC emergency response team dispatched to Louisiana in the aftermath of Hurricane Katrina.

Because it operates in 25 countries around the world, the reach and scope of the IRC's works is quite dramatic. But, at the end of the day, it all comes down to individual people getting the help they need when it matters most.

Helping the IRC is about reaching out to a child in a crowded refugee camp who, along with her mother, fled Darfur when armed men burned their village and slaughtered her father in a wanton killing spree of genocide.

It's about throwing a lifeline to a mother in war-torn Sierra Leone desperately trying to keep her infant son alive until food and help arrives. Or helping a father and daughter in Indonesia, staring at a heap of mud and rubble that once was their home until it and the rest of their family were swept out to sea.

That is why I am urging you to join the IRC by making a gift of $20, $35, $50 or more to help pull more people trapped in desperate circumstances across the line to safety.

Your generosity will be deeply felt . . .

. . . every time the IRC helps put a roof over a family that has walked hundreds of miles in search of safety . . .

. . . every time we help vaccinate an infant against preventable, deadly childhood diseases that run rampant in refugee communities . . .

. . . every time we rescue a child soldier who has been abducted and forced to fight, and help that child slowly recover.

I told you that the IRC acts with courage and conviction at the point of emergency. But, that's not the whole story. Some of the most vitally important work IRC does comes in the aftermath of emergency situations.

There's no better example than Rwanda. The IRC did far more than join in the global response to the devastating genocide in that nation. IRC teams have stayed in Rwanda for over a decade, playing a pivotal role in rebuilding civil society and promoting a process of justice and reconciliation to help the people of that deeply-troubled nation find a path out of the horror.

So, I hope you can see why your support is so urgently needed. Nonetheless, before answering my request, you probably want evidence that your support will make a real difference. On that score, you don't have to take my word for it.

Publications such as *Newsweek, Consumers Digest, SmartMoney*, and *Forbes* magazines have repeatedly ranked the International Rescue Committee as one of America's top charities. *SmartMoney* even says that if you support the IRC, you will "get the most bang for your donated buck."

> That's because 90 cents of every dollar the IRC spends goes directly to helping refugees and others in desperate need.

Charity watchdog groups give the IRC high marks for fiscal efficiency as well. The American Institute for Philanthropy give the IRC an "A," and Charity Navigator, a respected charity rating Web site gives the IRC 3 stars, putting it above and beyond most charities' ratings. And the IRC meets all the standards set for charities by the Better Business Bureau Wise Giving Alliance.

Let me close by returning to my personal commitment to the IRC. I am not writing to ask you to support an organization with which I have a passing familiarity. I am urging you to join me in helping sustain the work of a group to which I am deeply committed.

From the vantage point of a journalist who has seen the IRC in action—as a father whose daughter has helped to carry out its life-saving work—and now, as a member of the IRC Board who closely follows all of its many humanitarian interventions around the world, I have a deep and abiding faith in the IRC's unique understanding of what needs to be done, its capacity to act, and its ability to get the job done.

So I hope you will accept my personal invitation and support this extraordinary organization. Please send in your contribution to the International Rescue Committee today.

Sincerely,

Tom Brokaw
Co-Chair, Board of Overseers

P.S. To get the most up-to-date information about the IRC's activities around the world, please visit www.theIRC.org. And please join the IRC by sending your donation today.

> You have 30 minutes to pack everything you own. If you and your family can't carry it on your backs, it will have to stay behind.
> Look around one last time because you may never return to this home again.

And be careful what route you take. Choose wrong and your family could perish by nightfall . . .

Dear Friend,

You may have trouble imagining what it would be like to be driven from your home.

But, for too many people in our world, experiencing the fear, pain, and agony of such an event is not an act of imagination. It is too vivid a memory.

That's certainly true for two children from Kosovo, aged 16 and 17. To protect their identities, I'll call them Mira and Lindita.

"It was night when we heard gunshots from outside," said Lindita. Serb troops and police had entered her village near Pec in western Kosovo. They were yelling 'Get out, get out.' We ran outside, and across the bodies of our neighbors."

Mira guesses that she saw almost 200 dead, most shot in the back. She and Lindita were ordered to leave, and did, driving their old car to the mountains. But their terror was far from over. Within days, Serbs came again. Once again, they had to flee, this time to another village.

And still no peace: *again* it happened. They were asleep when, without warning, a shell collapsed the roof of the house. Again, they ran. Only after all this did they finally reach an Albanian refugee camp.

Mira and Lindita are far from unique. For this nightmare is one that has visited hundreds of thousands of people in Kosovo . . .

. . . *but not just in Kosovo*. This is a horror story repeated *daily* around the world. It is, in fact, happening to someone, somewhere, even as you read this letter.

From Asia to Africa to South America, *millions* of people have been driven from their homes, and are now refugees. For them, everything they've ever known—home, friends, communities, and very often some or all of their family—is lost. Frequently, they have witnessed acts of unspeakable brutality as well.

In the face of such events, disturbing questions confront each and every one of us.

Which of these people is to perish? Who among them is less worthy of life? Who among them should we write off, turn our backs on, and walk away from? Which man, woman, or child should we consign to hopelessness and perhaps death?

At the IRC, we reject the very premise behind these questions—and recognize the moral burden every decent human being has to never make such choices.

If you share our values, I urge you to join the International Rescue Committee. Our mission is to help *all* refugees and internally displaced people, providing whatever assistance they need, for as long as they need it.

Founded almost 70 years ago at the impetus of Dr. Albert Einstein, the IRC is the world's largest and oldest organization exclusively devoted to helping refugees around the world find sanctuary . . . *and* find an opportunity to build new lives.

The IRC is much more than a "disaster relief organization." Our goal is not only to help refugees the moment we learn of their plight, but to *continue* with that help right up until they have successfully established new lives . . . either after repatriation to their former homes—as is happening now in Kosovo—or after beginning afresh in new lands.

But right now, we face a staggering challenge. Even as we continue to respond to the ongoing situation in Kosovo, we struggle to maintain our vital refugee programs in nearly 30 countries. This effort has put extraordinary demands on our financial resources. To continue helping others, we need help from *you*.

That's why I'm writing today to ask you to help us by immediately sending us *your most generous tax-deductible contribution possible*.

From global emergency relief to well-planned resettlement assistance, the International Rescue Committee is the world's leading advocate for refugees. The IRC is one of the few humanitarian organizations with an ability to quickly meet refugee emergencies worldwide. We are often among the first international aid agencies to arrive on the scene. We provide critical medical services, food and shelter, as well as public health and sanitation assistance essential to saving lives.

Once a crisis is stabilized, we help refugees cope through training, education, and income-generating and self-reliance projects. The IRC also resettles 8,500 legally admitted refugees annually in the United States through 16 offices around the country.

On a daily basis, hundreds of thousands of refugees feel the impact of the IRC's work.

If you could be with our teams in the field, you would see painful situations and heart-breaking examples of people tormented by cruelty, intolerance, and inhumanity.

But, you would see something else as well—something more uplifting and positive. You would see the IRC delivering hope in circumstances that might be seen as hopeless.

And you would come away from your visit to IRC projects with an enormous respect for the strength, courage and determination of the refugees we serve and a clear understanding of the role concerned people like you play in making our work possible.

It would require a small book just to describe our vast array of programs. Consider a few examples:

- In Northern Uganda, children—children ages 8–11 years old!— have been "conscripted" (that is, kidnapped) into warfare by the "Lord's Resistance Army." Thousands have eventually escaped their captivity, returning home traumatized, bereft, and alone. The IRC is there to help them, providing everything from emergency shelter to long-term education and support.

- In Azerbaijan, we've helped refugees—forced from their homes in Nagorno Karabakh—build temporary mud-brick homes by providing windows, doors, and roofs. These last far longer than tents, yet cost just one-sixth of what a prefabricated house costs . . . and these components can later be used to restore houses once the refugees do return to their homelands.

- In Guinea, the refugee school system we support has *72,000 students*, ranging from nursery school through adult education. And in Pakistan, we support 27 schools that serve more than 12,000 refugee Afghan girls.

Our Health Program in Sudan is providing assistance to 20,000 people displaced by war, while in the Republic of Congo IRC-rehabilitated hospitals are serving *400,000* people. In the Ivory Coast, we're training Liberian refugee women to build their own homes. And in Europe and the U.S., among refugees who've been permitted to immigrate, we operate ongoing programs providing job training, housing assistance and more.

All in all, our programs help *hundreds of thousands of people* each year in a score of nations. But this year—a year of exceptional need—our resources are, as I said before, stretched tight.

That's why it is more important than ever that you join in supporting our work, that you stand with us in promising those who have been driven from their homes that they will never be abandoned, never left alone.

On behalf of the staff of the IRC and, most importantly, on behalf of the individual refugees your gift will help us reach, I urge you to join the IRC.

I implore you to dig deep, and send the most generous gift—be it $20 or $200—that you can possibly afford. Rest assured that whatever you send will be *instantly* put to work helping refugees around the world. Thank you for caring.

Sincerely,

Reynold Levy
President

P.S. Remember, too, that we do our work with legendary frugality, as both *Consumer's Digest* and *Smart Money* magazines have noted.

P.P.S. Terrific news! Our latest financial report shows that the IRC has further reduced its administrative and fundraising costs. Now 93 cents of every dollar we spend directly supports refugee services.

NOTES

INTRODUCTION

1. These data are drawn from *Giving USA 2007: The Annual Report on Philanthropy for the Year 2006* (Indianapolis, IN: Giving USA Foundation, 2007).
2. Virginia A. Hodgkinson et al., *Nonprofit Almanac, 1996–1997: Dimensions of the Independent Sector* (San Francisco: Jossey-Bass, 1996).
3. Ibid.

CHAPTER 1

1. Russ Alan Prince and Lewis Schiff, *The Middle-Class Millionaire: The Rise of the New Rich and How They Are Changing America* (New York: Doubleday, 2008).
2. Thomas J. Stanley and William D. Danko, *The Millionaire Next Door: The Surprising Secrets of America's Wealthy* (Atlanta: Longstreet Press, 1996).
3. *Business Week,* October 2, 2006, 12.
4. Jeffrey Sachs, "The Power of One: Sharing the Wealth," *Time,* May 21, 2007.

CHAPTER 2

1. Kenneth N. Dayton, *The Stages of Giving* (Washington, D.C.: The Independent Sector, Part of the *Conversations with Leaders Series,* 1999).

2. Noelle Barton and Peter Panepento, "A Surge in Assets: Donor-Advised Funds Are Growing Exponentially," *Chronicle of Philanthropy*, May 3, 2007, 7, 10, and 12.

3. Daisey Maxey, "Ranks of Rich in U.S. Grow at Faster Pace," *Wall Street Journal*, June 28, 2007, D6.

4. Mark J. Penn with E. Kinney Zalasne, *Microtrends: The Small Forces behind Tomorrow's Big Changes* (New York: Hachette Book Group, 2007), 224–229.

5. Katie Hafner, "Google Options Make Masseuse a Multimillionaire," *New York Times*, November 12, 2007.

6. *Forbes*, March 24, 2008, 146.

7. See also *Chronicle of Philanthropy*, January 25, 2007, 7, 9–12.

8. Ibid.

9. Alan S. Blinder, "The Under-Taxed Kings of Private Equity," *New York Times,* July 29, 2007.

10. Claude Rosenberg, Jr., *Wealthy and Wise: How You And America Can Get the Most Out of Your Giving* (Boston: Little, Brown and Company, 1994).

11. Franz Fanon, *The Wretched of the Earth* (Paris, 1961).

12. Francis Ostrower, *Why the Wealthy Give: The Culture of Elite Philanthropy* (Princeton, NJ: Princeton University Press, 1995), 10–11.

13. Ibid.

14. *The Lincoln Center Corporate Fund Annual Report: 2007.*

15. John Gardner, *Self Renewal: The Individual and the Innovative Society* (New York: W.W. Norton and Company, 1981).

16. Chris Matthews, *Life's a Campaign: What Politics Has Taught Me about Friendship, Rivalry, Reputation and Success* (New York: Random House, 2007), 14–15.

17. Arthur C. Brooks, *Who Really Cares: The Surprising Truth about Compassionate Conservatism* (New York: Basic Books, 2006); and Arthur C. Brooks, "Why Giving Makes You Happy," *New York Sun,* December 28–30, 2007.

18. Herbert Allen, "Gold in the Ivory Tower," *New York Times,* December 21, 2007; and Todd G. Bucholz "Better Begging: When Wealthy Universities Ask for Money, Why Do We Say Yes?" *Wall Street Journal,* December 7, 2007.

CHAPTER 4

1. "Projection 2007: Sponsorship Growth to Increase for Fifth Straight Year," *Arts Insights* (December 2006).
2. *Giving USA 2007: The Annual Report on Philanthropy for the Year 2006* (Indianapolis, IN: Giving USA Foundation, 2007).
3. Dwight Burlingame and Patricia Frishoff, "How Does Firm Size Affect Corporate Philanthropy?" in *Corporate Philanthropy at the Crossroads*, Dwight F. Burlingame and Dennis R. Young, eds. (Bloomington: Indiana University Press, 1996).
4. Reynold Levy, *Give and Take: A Candid Account of Corporate Philanthropy* (Boston: Harvard Business School Press, 1999), 173.
5. Ibid., 191–192.
6. Herb Greenberg, "How Values Embraced by a Company May Enhance That Company's Value," *Wall Street Journal*, October 27–28, 2007.
7. Ibid.
8. Joel L. Fleishman, *The Foundation: A Great American Secret—How Private Wealth Is Changing the World* (New York: Public Affairs, 2007).
9. Ben Wildavsky, "Generous to a Fault? A Close Look at Giving—Book Review—*The Foundation*," *Wall Street Journal*, January 11, 2007.

CHAPTER 6

1. Bill Gross as quoted in Robert Frank, "The Buzz: Best of WSJ.com's Money Blogs," *Wall Street Journal*, August 4–5, 2007.
2. Stephanie Strom, "Many Dismissing 'Donor Fatigue' as Myth: Despite Disasters, Charities Say '05 Giving Held Steady," *New York Times*, April 30, 2006.
3. Juan Gonzalez, "Randalls for Rich," *Daily News*, February 23, 2007; and Timothy Williams, "Lawsuit Seeks to Break Deal over Use of Randalls Island," *New York Times*, June 15, 2007.
4. Jacques Steinberg, "Yale Returns $20 Million to an Unhappy Patron," *New York Times*, March 15, 1995; and Ryan E. Smith, "The Bass Grant: Why Yale gave $20 Million Back," *Yale Herald*, March 24, 1995.

5. David E. Rosenbaum, "Museum Insisted on Control of $38 Million Gift," *The New York Times*, February 6, 2002; and "Who is Catherine Reynolds?", *60 Minutes*, CBS, August 24, 2003.
6. Stephanie Strom, "Nonprofit Groups Draw a Line at Some Donors: Saying No Thank You to Corporations with Policies at Odds with the Mission," *New York Times*, January 28, 2007.

CHAPTER 9

1. Lester M. Salamon, *The Global Associational Revolution: The Rise of the Third Sector on the World Scene* (Baltimore: Johns Hopkins University Institute for Policy Studies, occasional paper, no. 15, April 1993).
2. Souren Melikian, "The Vision Behind the Louvre's Metamorphosis: Director Takes Globalist Path," *International Herald Tribune*, September 9–10, 2006; Alan Riding, "The Louvre's Art: Priceless. The Louvre's Name: Expensive," *New York Times*, March 7, 2007; Nicolai Ouroussoff, "A Vision in the Desert," *New York Times*, February 4, 2007.
3. Ibid.
4. Tamar Lewin, "Universities Compete for Overseas Outposts," *New York Times*, February 10, 2008.
5. Andrew Ross Sorkin, "How to Show that You're No Gordon Gekko," *New York Times*, March 25, 2007.
6. Victor E. Frankl, *Man's Search for Meaning* (Boston: Beacon Press, 2006), xiv–xv, preface to the 1992 edition.
7. Arthur Brooks, "Why Giving Makes You Happy," *New York Sun*, December 28–30, 2007.
8. Herb Greenberg, "How Values Embraced by a Company May Enhance that Company's Value," *Wall Street Journal*, October 27–28, 2007.
9. John W. Wright, ed., *The New York Times Almanac of Record: 2008* (New York: Penguin, 2008), 815–816.

INDEX